The Nature of Divine Relationships

by

Pastor Ralph Dawkins

"And I will give them an heart to know me, that I am the LORD: and they shall be my people, and I will be their God: for they shall return unto me with their whole heart."
Jeremiah 24:7

Biblical scriptures in this book are taken from the King James Version, Amplified, and New International Version, unless otherwise noted.

The Nature of Divine Relationships
2nd Printing 01/09

ISBN: 978-1502526656

To contact the author and publisher or to request permission to reproduce any parts or sections of this book, please contact:

Pastor Ralph Dawkins
Christian House of Prayer – San Angelo
333 West Avenue C, San Angelo, Texas 76903

Acknowledgments

I would like to thank my Lord and Savior Jesus Christ for giving me such a profound revelation about the relationships the Father established around each of us to make our lives special. He is the air I breathe, the song I sing and I owe Him everything.

To my wife for life, Gwen, who has stayed with me these 27 years through thick and thin. You are my best friend, my cherished companion and without you, this book would have no validity, for God has divinely blessed me to have you as my wife. I love You BBG!

To my sons, Aaron and Moshe, another demonstration of what divine relationships is all about. I am honored to be your dad and it is my desire to withhold no good thing from you.

To my mother, Willia Mae Dawkins, thank you for loving me, putting up with me and understanding me when no one else could. You have taught me and showed me love that goes beyond words. I love you.

To my sisters, Jean Harris and Rene Pulliam and their families, thank you for your love and prayers and the spirit of family you have poured into me, even when time and distance didn't allow us to be together as often as we would have liked. Love you later, Love you lots!

To my bishop and his wife, Bishop Nathaniel and Valerie Holcomb of the Christian House of Prayer Ministries, Cathedral of Central Texas, Killeen, Texas for their love, guidance and anointed example of what God meant when He said, "I will give you pastors after mine own heart" (Jeremiah 3:15).

To my covenant brothers, Pastor Fred Moore, Austin, Texas and Dr. Jovaster Witcher, Waco, Texas - your prayers, friendship and accountability are more precious than silver.

To Pastor Kenneth and Regina Scott, Birmingham, Alabama for encouraging me to take the step of faith to write this book and guiding me through the process.

To the people behind the scenes, who helped make this dream project come true, our assistant, Ms Denise Jones (What would we do without Denise?), Antwain Gooding for your creative artwork on the covers, and Mrs. Sandra Gray, editor *par excellence.*

Lastly, to the staff and precious membership of Christian House of Prayer – San Angelo, thank you for allowing me to shepherd you and for your support and encouragement. You make being a pastor a joy!

Foreword

My favorite text in all the Bible is found in St. Matthew 16:13-19. Jesus is asking His disciples, *"Whom do men say that I the Son of man am?"* The disciples began with John the Baptist, Elijah, Jeremiah or just one of the prophets. Then, Jesus asked the disciples, "*Whom say ye that I am?"* Peter answers, "*The Christ, Son of the Living God."* Pastor Dawkins, through revelation from the Father and illumination of the Spirit has captured the heart of the Lord as it relates to our relationship to the Godhead and consequently our relationship to one another.

The first of all the commandments Jesus quoted is, "...Hear, O Israel, the Lord our God is one Lord: And thou shalt love the Lord with all thy heart,... And the second is namely this, Thou shalt love thy neighbor as thyself..." (Mark 12:29-31).

These two are the greatest commandments and both are the foundation for all true relationships. Pastor Dawkins' book on "The Nature of Divine Relationships" gives us God's laws, which are fixed principles but also the pragmatics of the mind of Christ in how they are to be lived out in everyday life.

The old adage "No Man is an Island" speaks to the very issue of relationship. No one can live successfully without understanding this important concept. "The

Nature of Divine Relationships" is so impacting because it brings us back to the original maker and His design from the beginning. When something does not work right, we need to take it back to its maker. The Nature of Divine Relationships does just that, it brings us back to our Creator, and what He had in mind from the beginning.

Bishop Nate Holcomb
Covenant Connections International Inc.

CONTENTS

Section III

Introduction

> *"...the heir, as long as he is a child, differeth nothing from a servant, though he be lord of all; But is under tutors and governors until the time appointed of the Father. Even so we, when we were children, were in bondage under the elements of the world: but when the fullness of time was come, God sent forth his Son, made from a woman, made under the law, to redeem them that were under the law that they might receive the Adoption of Sons. And because ye are sons, God hath sent forth the Spirit of his Son into your hearts, crying Abba, Father. Wherefore thou art no more a servant, but a son; and if a son, then an heir of God through Christ."*
>
> Galatians 4:1-7

A few years ago, the Lord had me to take a very close look at this scripture. I began to realize that all of what the Father has provided for us is based on the nature of our relationship to Him.

In this one scripture, He has transitioned us from being a child to a son and from a son to an heir of God through Jesus Christ. There is a great revelation to be exposed as you explore the Bible and discover that, we as Christians, have a divine inheritance awaiting us through a divine relationship with God.

A revelation is defined as (1) Something revealed, (2) The disclosure of something not previously known or realized and (3) A manifestation of a divine will or truth. The nature of divine relationships has become a revelation from God that has literally changed my life. The discovery of reasons regarding who, how and why certain relationships in my life have taken place, has unfolded into a whole new understanding of God's purpose for my life.

Throughout this book, I will refer to what I call, "Genesis Principles". These principles are given to establish a point of reference during the creation process that is present and active in our everyday lives today. I pray that this book will be a blessing to you and prompt you to closely examine the relationships in and around your life. Enjoy!

Exploring The Nature of Divine Relationships

I received an e-mail from a friend a few years ago that said..."*People come into your life for 1) a reason, 2) a season, or 3) a lifetime.*" It is important to know and understand the differences.

When someone is in your life for a reason, it is usually to meet a need you have expressed outwardly or inwardly. They are there for the reason you need them to be. Then, without any necessary wrongdoing on your part or theirs, something happens to bring the relationship to an end. Sometimes they walk away, sometimes they move to another city, sometimes they die. Either way, the purpose of the relationship has been fulfilled and you both move on. Years later, you may not remember their name or face, but once reminded of them, you can instantly go back to the details of your encounter.

Genesis 8:22 says,

> *"While the earth remaineth, seedtime and harvest, and cold and heat, and summer and winter, and day and night shall not cease."*

This Genesis Principle speaks about the seasons of life that affect everyone.

When a person comes into your life for a season, it is because it is time for you or them to grow, share or learn. When they come, they may bring you enlightenment and experiences that are invaluable for their future as well as yours.

Some seasons last longer than others and as the season moves on, so will this unique person in your life. Should you encounter this person again, you will be able to remember some of the details without being reminded; you can recall the face or features of their character because you have shared some experiences together.

Lifetime relationships teach you lifetime lessons; which are things you must build upon in order to have a solid emotional and spiritual foundation. The ability to embrace these relationships are important to every person I know. Lifetime relationships don't need any assistance. It is amazing how many details you can recall (names, dates, places and faces) twenty or even thirty years later.

Lifetime relationships teach you lifetime lessons...

Two things you need to know before we journey into this subject matter:

1) The truths regarding divine relationships are universal. In other words, they work whether you are a Christian or not, they speak to every area of our lives, and they are ever present around us, whether we apply them or not.

2) Secondly, the concepts mentioned in this book can be applied to secular work relationships as well as those in the church and in your family. Let the reader beware however, after reading this book, you will begin to look more closely at the people and relationships around you, and you will be surprised at what you see.

As I began to search the Word of God for answers and insights to understand the nature of divine relationships, three key points jumped out at me.

Here's what the Lord showed me...

1. The Bible is a book about relationships.
2. Nearly every parable or story spoken by Jesus was about relationships (including those about money).
3. The Father has a need that only we, as His children can fulfill. That's right! In all of His omnipotence, His omnipresence and His omniscience, He has a need, and that need is to have His children reconciled to Him.

The Father calls us His children, His beloved, His sons and daughters, His seed, and His heirs. Our prosperity is tied to our relationship with Him. It is a prosperity that was promised before we were even born. Healing is tied to our relationship with our Heavenly Father. It was paid IN FULL at Calvary. Deliverance is tied to our relationship with Him. It was implemented when we accepted Jesus Christ as Lord and personal Savior.

Did you know that Heaven is about relationships? Yes. Even Heaven will come to one climactic celebration when the relationship of the ages is restored (Revelation 21:17). Your marriage, your ministry and your manhood (or womanhood) is tied to your relationship with God because they are divinely inspired by God.

Many people in and out of the body of Christ do not know that God has their money, their spouse and their deliverance in His hands and He wants to give them much more, but He longs for the relationship with them first. We were created as social beings, so it is no small wonder that our marriage, ministries and effectiveness in management seems to go more smoothly when our social forces are in proper balance.

When people embrace God with an ulterior motive (getting more money, finding a spouse, or getting out of a mess), they miss the bigger picture, which is stated so eloquently in Matthew 6:33,

> *"Seek ye first the kingdom of God and His righteousness, all these things will be added to you."*

Everything that God creates is associated with a relationship of some type.

Consider this... Everything that God creates is associated with a relationship of some type. Our solar system is held together by an intricate association of planets and stars and moons.

God did this purposely. On our planet, all of nature (land, sea and air) is based on a relationship with the other elements surrounding us. (Gen 2:7 and John 20:22).

I call this the **Principle of Agreement.** The word *Agreement* has its root in the Greek language is the word: *Sumphoneo* - Where we get our English words

1. Synonym - one or more words or expressions of the same language that have the same or nearly the same meaning in some or all senses
2. Symposium - where people come together to discuss a particular subject
3. Symbiosis – where two living organism live in mutual interdependence

4. Symphysis – where you have a growing together – like bones growing (fusing) back together

I will address more on the Principle of Agreement later in the book.

The point here is that there is nothing more important in life than having an intimate relationship with the Father God, regardless of what level you are at as a Christian. Think of it this way... When children have a healthy relationship with their father, they are less likely to commit crime. They do better in school and are less likely to have issues involving teenage pregnancy. If it's true in the natural, is it possible that it is true in the spiritual?

A relationship is defined as the "state or quality of being connected" (i.e. A kinship or association). When something is considered "Divine", it carries the connotation that God is involved or inspires it. Well... A Divine Relationship (Dawkins Translation) is a "Kinship or association inspired by God". That seems too simple doesn't it? The real paradox is that sometimes in the Nature of Divine Relationships, God doesn't make sense.

Consider how He dealt with Noah, Hosea, and Jonah. Why would God want to make an investment into a people who were in sin, stiff-necked, hard-hearted and rebellious? To our logical mind, none of them were worth saving because they had nothing to give. His actions didn't make sense to me either when out of all the good people I knew as I was growing up in Brooklyn, New York, He would speak to me and deliver me, even though, I too, had nothing to offer Him. Why would He love someone who consistently toyed with Him, spoke one thing but said another concerning Him and would call on Him only when I needed His help?

In all of His wisdom, God somehow looks beyond our infirmities and flaws and sees a person worth delivering and worthy of making an investment in us.

PRINCIPLES TO LIVE BY

- The Bible is a book about relationships
- Nearly every parable and story spoken by Jesus was about relationship (including those about money)
- The Father has a need that only we (as His children) can fulfill. In all of His omnipotence, His omnipresence and His omniscience, He has a need, and that need is to have His children reconciled to Him
- Everything that God creates is associated with a relationship of some type
- When someone is in your life for a reason, it is usually to meet a need you have expressed outwardly or inwardly
- When a person comes into your life for a season, it is because it is time for you or them to grow, share or learn
- Lifetime relationships teach you lifetime lessons; those things you must build upon in order to have a solid emotional foundation
- A Divine relationship (Dawkins Translation) is a "Kinship or association inspired by God".

Section 1

Every Healthy Relationship Must Be...

Clearly Defined

Matthew 16:13-16
"When Jesus came into the coasts of Caesarea Philippi, he asked his disciples saying, Whom do men say that I the Son of man am? And they said, Some say that thou art John the Baptist: some, Elias; and others, Jeremiah or one of the prophets. He saith unto them, But whom do ye say that I am? And Simon Peter answered and said, Thou art the Christ, the Son of the Living God"

Every relationship (with God or man) must be clearly defined in order for the relationship to continue and grow. Misjudging the nature of any relationship can lead you to be frustrated, misunderstood, hurt, angry or disappointed.

In Matthew 16:13-20, Jesus knows that the future of Christianity rests on the revelation Peter has of the Christ. I believe all of Heaven stood poised, anticipating Peter's answer. If he gives the wrong answer, Jesus would have to look for someone else who has received the revelation of who He really is; if he answers correctly, then Jesus could bestow <u>authority</u>, <u>access</u> and <u>covenant</u> to Peter and the others. Notice that it doesn't matter who other men say He is, what is most important here is that Peter has a clear definition of who Jesus is.

Thankfully Peter answers correctly. Notice Jesus' response (verse 17-19),

> *"Blessed are you Simon Bar-jona: for flesh and blood hath not revealed it to thee but my Father which is in heaven. And I say also unto thee, That thou art Peter, and upon this rock I will build my church; and the gates of hell shall not prevail against it. And I will give unto thee the <u>keys of the Kingdom of Heaven</u>: and whatsoever thou shalt bind on earth shall be bound in heaven: and whatsoever thou shalt loose on earth shall be loosed in heaven."*

Jesus could not empower nor entrust Peter with the keys to the Kingdom of Heaven (signifying access), nor give him a new name (signifying covenant), nor authority (signifying power) to bind and loose, without first clearly defining the nature of their relationship. Peter's answer also speaks to our generation. I can see why the Catholic Church puts so much emphasis on Peter, making him their first bishop - he was the first one to clearly articulate the clear definitions between us and our Savior, *"Thou art the Christ"*.

The church, however, is built on the revelation, not on the man. God gives revelation continually as we continue to pursue a relationship with Him. This is why prayer and worship is so important. It puts us in a continual posture to pursue Him.

There is a Genesis principle I call the **Principle of Identification**. It simply states that in the nature of divine relationships, an identification must be established in order for the relationship to be blessed. In the book of Genesis God speaks to Jacob and says,

> ***"I am the Lord God of Abraham thy father, and the God of Isaac***: *the land whereon thou liest, to thee will I give it, and to thy seed.... And behold, I am with thee, and I will keep thee in all the places whither thou goest, and I will bring thee*

*again into this land, for **I will not leave thee, until I have done that which I have spoken to thee of**.*"

Genesis 28:13-15, (emphasis added)

This principle is laced throughout the Bible as a statement God wants firmly planted in or hearts. In Genesis, whatever He created, He gave a <u>purpose</u> and gave a <u>name</u>. For example, in Genesis 1

V5) "And God called the light Day, and the darkness he called Night."
V8) "And God called the firmament Heaven."
V10) "And God called the dry [land] Earth; and the gathering together of the waters called he Seas..."

He identifies who He is <u>before</u> imparting the blessing and it is vitality important for us to identify who He is in our lives.

Later in chapter one, before He created Adam, He had a purpose for His design. His intent was to create man in "our image, after our likeness; and let them have dominion over the fish, fowls cattle and every thing that creepeth". Then He transfers the same authority and dominion to Adam (2:19b) "and whatsoever Adam called every living creature, that was the name thereof, including Woman in verse 23.

When one party is changing and the other party refuses to change, that relationship is in jeopardy of being weakened.

All of these exist in a relationship dynamic and the same is true for us today. Clearly defined relationships have a purpose and therefore we must give it a name. Nothing that God created is ambiguous and without identification – everything has a purpose and a name.

Every relationship that is alive and growing goes through change. When one party changes and the other party refuses to change, that relationship is in jeopardy of being weakened. In your Christian walk, you should be changing "from glory to glory" and "from faith to faith", day by day. Consider the martyrs in early Christendom; when they faced death, they would honorably lay down their lives for the relationship and the furtherance of the gospel. They would endure humiliation and persecution for the sake of the relationship, not just as a good work or a noble deed.

Many Christians believe that their relationship with God does not need to be developed or be clearly manifested to the public. Jesus taught us that,

> *"God is not a secret to be kept. We're going public with this, as public as a city on a hill. Keep open house; be generous with your lives. By opening up to others, you'll prompt people to open up with God..."*
>
> Matthew 5:14-16 (MSG)

Let me help dispel a churchy notion. Just because a person goes to church on a Sunday morning or does volunteer work at the church, does not substitute for the one-on-one time God wants to spend with you. Most people I know who are doing well in ministry, marriage or career have a continual openness in expressing the nature of their relationship with others.

I believe everyone reading this book should confirm their relationship with God. **Have you confessed Him as your personal Lord and Savior?** *Are you His child or not*? It is time to settle the matter. Ambiguously defined relationships usually results in someone getting hurt or disappointed.

> *"...Not everyone that saith Lord, Lord, shall inherit the kingdom of heaven; but he that doeth the will of my Father which is in heaven. Many will say in that day, Lord, Lord, have we not prophesied in thy name? And in thy name cast out devils? And in thy name done many wonderful works? And then I will profess unto them,* ***I never knew***

> ***you**: depart from me, ye that work iniquity".*
>
> Matthew 7:21-23 (emphasis added)

Many times He will remind us who He is and the relationship He wants with us <u>before</u> He gives a command...

This scripture makes it pretty clear. It is possible for a person to cast out devils, prophesy and do wonderful works and miss the opportunity to go to heaven. **How?** By never coming into a true, clearly defined relationship with the Father.

Have you ever looked through the Bible and noticed how many times God would say, "*I am the Lord thy God*", or "*I will be their God, and they will be my people*"? Many times He will remind us of who He is and the relationship He wants with us <u>before</u> He gives a command, speaks through a prophet or performs a miracle. He will make declarative statements like, "I AM" (whatever you need Him to be)"; He will first clearly establish who He is to us.

On a more practical note, take the case of a young man or woman who misunderstood the nature of their relationship. Statements like, "I just wanted to be your <u>friend</u>, or "I thought you loved me" or the classic line from the '70's, "I love you so much that I am willing to let you go", are usually spoken by those who have missed the mark on defining the nature of their relationship. Failure to clearly define basic relationships in day to day living can result in unwanted pregnancies, abuse and mistrust. If a young engaged couple does not clearly define their relationship on a continual basis, they deny themselves the opportunity to solidify the foundation of their impending marriage.

Let's look at three separate environments common to most of us to see the importance of clearly defining the relationships around us.

LET' S GO TO CHURCH

How many times has misjudging the church relationship between a pastor and a member has led to disappointment or an unrepentant early exit from church membership? I cannot tell you how many times I have had Christians come into my office who are not members of my church to discuss an issue. One of the first questions I will ask is, *"Have you discussed this matter with your pastor?"* Eighty percent of the respondents say, "No!" For any number of reasons, Christians will not turn to their own clergy person for an answer, they would rather go to someone else to discuss the sensitive matter instead of taking it to their clergyman, the person who God has ordained to pray for them and shepherd their soul. If you're not careful, this type of dynamic can backfire on you because it crosses the line of spiritual authority and relationships, both between the pastor and the member and pastor to another pastor.

Are you easily impressed by the outward demonstrated spirituality of someone in your church? I used to be, but not any longer. I have learned over the years that everything that glitters is not gold. Every person that walks into your church declaring how much they can do, and what they know, can deceive even the most seasoned church leader.

When new ministers come into our church to register their spiritual gift, I allow a certain period of time to transpire before using them or giving them any responsibility. This season is given to them to allow our relationship to be developed. Because we live in a performance based society, people will come into the church with high ambition to do things, however, if they have not caught the heart of the pastor nor the vision of the church, they can actually hinder the effectiveness of the ministry or misuse the authority given to them and cause hurt.

In our church, my wife and I make it a point to try to meet every new member that connects with our ministry. We sit in every New Members class (as time permits) and explain in no uncertain terms the vision for the church and what is deemed as appropriate or inappropriate behavior. It may come across as being strict or too straightforward but in these days of deception, I believe it is important to clearly define church membership roles and operational procedures so that there is no room for offense.

I make it clear that expectations placed on us go both ways. I tell them that if it is unethical for the Reverend (me) to have a girlfriend on the side, drink, party, smoke and lie, the same holds true for them. I believe it is unfair to hold church members to a standard of behavior that ministers are not willing to embrace for themselves.

The bottom line question is… "Am I <u>your</u> pastor?" I have learned over the years that within my church there are three levels of relationships that are analogous to the tabernacle (Outer Court, Inner Court and Holy of Holies). I have the congregation (Outer Court), the membership (Inner Court) and the staff (Holy of Holies). It is important that pastors know the difference; otherwise you will be set up for disappointment and discouragement.

There are matters of responsibility and confidentiality that are imparted into Inner Court staff people that Outer Court congregation people are not given. In terms of support and commitment, staff members are expected to take the lead in doing those things that I have shared with them in staff meetings or in-gatherings.

Things like tithing, consistent attendance in Bible Study or prayer and serving have become a benchmark that determines their commitment and loyalty, before any further expectation is manifested.

Pastors must realize that they may not be the pastor for everyone who visits or comes into their church. Some people who come to your church regularly only come to say, "Amen", feel good and be friendly, but as soon as a strong Word is ministered or a challenge is presented, they disappear and will strangely reappear when the challenge has left. You cannot place much investment in them because the foundation of the relationship is surface and cannot withstand anything more than curiosity and pleasantries.

Things like tithing, consistent attendance in Bible Study or Intercessory Prayer and faithful serving, have become a benchmark that determines their commitment and loyalty, before any further expectation is manifested. Once a visitor senses a "spiritual connection", and have embraced the vision of the church, the heart of the pastor, and the spirit of the house, they are then ready to make the next step toward membership. For some, it is almost immediate, for others, it takes a while for them to be comfortable enough to embrace the heart of the church and the pastor.

Membership people are those who have embraced a deeper relationship that is more consistent. They call you "Pastor" and have an expectation for hearing the voice of the pastor. Jesus said,

> *"...the sheep follow him, <u>for they know his voice</u>, and a stranger will they not follow, but will flee from him; for they know not the voice of strangers."*
>
> John 10:4, 5 (emphasis added)

As they connect, their pronouns change from, *that* church, to *my* church; from *that* pastor to *my* pastor and from what *they* are doing to what *we* are doing. When this happens, they become more open to the worship and their work in the ministry is not as inconsistent as it used to be. They can embrace the vision of the local church and are open to serve and participate and be a part of the exciting things going on in the church. Most importantly, they connect with the other members of the church. They eventually take on the sense of belonging and ownership for things happening in the church. We often say that, "If you want to be a part, you must do your part!"

Have you ever heard the statement that in most churches, "Twenty percent of the people do eighty percent of the work, and give eighty percent of the financial support of the ministry"? It's true! As unfortunate as it may be, the reality is that until a person can wholeheartedly embrace the ministry as theirs, they normally will not make an investment beyond the definition of the relationship. Matthew 6:21 says,

> *"For where your treasure is, there will your heart be also".*

I have noticed over the years that when members get offended (for whatever reason), one of the first things to be withheld is their giving. This is because their heart toward the relationship of the ministry has changed, so consequently their investment will follow.

Then of course your staff (paid or volunteer) members are those trusted members in the church who have assumed certain responsibilities to support the work of the ministry. Every elder, deacon, trustee, board member, auxiliary and minister must clearly define the relationship among themselves as well as those above or beneath them. Deacons don't run the church, and board members don't dictate what the pastor should or should not preach! The role of the pastor is clearly defined in Jeremiah 3:15, which says,

> *"And I will give you pastors according to mine heart, which shall feed you with knowledge and understanding."*

In the church, people are intricately connected to support one another and worship together, just as the human body is interconnected. Ephesians 4:6 says,

> *"From whom the whole body fitly joined together and compacted by that which every joint supplieth, according to the effectual working in the measure of every part, maketh increase of the body unto the edifying of itself in love."*

When people get excited and throw out blanket statements like, "I love you" to me, I take it for what it is worth based on our clearly defined relationship. In Luke 6:46, Jesus says,

> *"And why call ye me Lord, Lord, and do not the things which I say?"*

I say, why say you love me, when our relationship is not at that level yet? Jesus said, "*If you love me, keep my commandments*". Am I right? It is important to establish trust in a person, before saying such things.

THE BLESSING OF A COVERING

> *"... Thou hast made a hedge about him, and about his house, and about all that he hath on every side? Thou hast*

> *blessed the work of his hand, and his substance is increased in the land.*
> Job 1: 10 (emphasis added)

In this scripture the word "hedge" in the Hebrew is the word, "*suwk*", which means to entwine like a fence or restraint. Here Satan himself explains to God that there is a supernatural covering around Job that he can neither pull down nor penetrate.

> *"And it shall come to pass, while my glory passeth by, that I will put thee in a clift of the rock, and I will "cover" thee with my hand while I pass by".*
> Exodus 33:22

In this scripture, the word "Cover" is the word, *Sakak,* which means to *entwine* as a screen, to fence in cover or protect. Each of these scriptures (and there are many more) indicate that God has established a "Divine Overshadowing" over our lives to protect or cover us. **Every Christian needs a covering**; someone whom they not only trust, but whom will also teach, correct, guide, protect and feed with knowledge and understanding.

We live in a town where there is a strong military community. As I see young Christians, single or married transfer into San Angelo, I get concerned for them as they "shop" for their next church home. It is dangerous ground, to be once under the "Canopy of God's protection" (Psalm 91) in one country, church, or shepherd and have to leave the comfort of that spiritual environment where you knew everyone. You were like family in that church. You received your blessings through that church and you learned and developed your character through that ministry.

How do you replace the people, the love and the special covering of that house? The answer is... You don't! You can never replace the church or those you had experiences with. Settle the matter! Those relationships were divinely orchestrated by God. You were there for that reason or season, and then its time to glean from those blessings and experiences and grow in the things you were taught and move on to your next level of relationships as God orchestrates.

There are many church organizations and associations in America that would love to bring young pastors under "their" covering. Pastors... beware. God wants you to come under the proper covering for your life and ministry. The danger here is the secularized "corporate takeover" mentality of the world that is influencing the church. If you are the pastor of a young prospering church, be careful with whom you connect. Many associations pull relationship-starved pastors for a fee.

There are many church organizations and associations in America that would love to bring young pastors under "their covering". Pastors... beware.

That's like having someone join your church for a fee. Oftentimes they lure you with the names of popular ministers they are affiliated with as though you will get to have one-on-one opportunities with them where they will share secrets of their success. Some own up to their promises, most don't!

This is not the nature of a shepherd, it is more like the nature of a hireling (John 10:11-13). A hireling is like a minister for hire. They can preach, or sing for a fee. However, once a relationship challenge comes, they flee because their motivation is monetary. Any monetary blessings given to your man or woman of God should be given not because of a requirement, but because the relationship is natural and you are divinely inspired to sow into those who cover you and bless you. Amen?

At every level of authority in the church, members as well as those in leadership must clearly define, "who is who" in their church and in their lives.

Over the years I have come to know and appreciate a few pastors with whom I have a "shoulder to shoulder" relationship. I count it a blessing to have such men and women of God in my life. What is so special about these "divine relationships" is that there is no cause for pretence; we don't try to impress one another with stories of how wonderful our church is, or how many people we have in our congregation. If I am experiencing difficult or perplexing situations, I have no fear of calling any one of these brothers and "vent" about the hell that I am going through; it is very therapeutic! Sometimes we laugh, sometimes we cry, sometimes we give one another an encouraging word. **We never preach to one another at these times, we just keep things real between us**.

Recently, I shared with a pastor-friend of mine what I was going through as a foundation member of our church became offended and left suddenly. Understand that I am usually a very up-tempo kind of guy. But this particular evening he could tell in my voice that something was going on. I poured out my feelings of, "Maybe it was my fault", "What could I have done to prevent this terrible parting" and "How could a foundation member leave the church that THEY helped get started, I felt betrayed". Woe is me! Do you know what he said? After laughing and apologizing for laughing and then laughing again. He welcomed me to the REAL world of ministry. He said, *"For a while there brother I didn't think you had a ministry because you never shared the tough and hurting side of your ministry with me. I was thinking to hold back on what I was sharing with you because you never shared the serious matters with me. But now that you are sharing, I know that our relationship is indeed a divine relationship, sent by God for both of us. You need to write your book brother."*

Wow… What an eye-opener! I feel for pastors who have trying experiences in their personal lives, family lives or their ministry lives and have no one to turn to for a Word or consolation. I thank God for my pastors Bishop Nate and Pastor Valerie Holcomb, Killeen, Texas.

…"Insight for Oversight". This is a no joke type of relationship that will bless anyone who understands and is tired of fake, pretentious, pseudo overseers…

They have set up Covenant Connections International (CCI), which is a network of some eighty plus churches - nationally and internationally – to advise, encourage, and provide resources to ministries and ministers who are seeking a divine relationship with people who are serious about the Father's business. He calls it "Insight for Oversight". This is a no joke type of relationship that will bless anyone who understands the importance of having someone speak into their lives and is tired of fake, pretentious, pseudo overseers whose motivation is money, prestige and power over small churches. He is my "Father in the Faith", who calls me "Son".

WHO'S YOUR DADDY?

There are probably thousands of young ministers who are currently looking for their "Father in the Faith", because without them, something is missing in their ministry. It is the reason why many ministers migrate from conference to conference, following who has the freshest anointing or who stirs them up the most. Every big name preacher is not your father in the faith! There has to be a spiritual connection established first; then you can determine if a clearly defined relationship has been orchestrated by God. Once it is established, you can say without any hesitation, "I have found my father and this is where I belong".

Every big name preacher is not your father in the faith! There has to be a spiritual connection established first...

ON THE HOMEFRONT

I believe that God does not want to have a platonic or distant relationship with man. He does not want to be professional with you nor become your colleague. Believe me, **we are not at His level.** He longs for a loving, nurturing relationship where He can reveal Himself to you and for you to reveal yourself to Him. The true nature of His being, which is that of a loving, caring, and sharing heavenly Father, is a life-changing discovery. The same is true in the family.

When roles in the family relationship are not clearly defined, it is like an accident waiting to happen. I can remember when I was dating my wife (then fiancée) she made the definition of our relationship very clear many times. "We are friends", was the response to my every attempt to cross the line. As we became friends, it was obvious that we had good chemistry but we were limited because "friends" don't do certain things with one another.

When parents don't clearly define the relationship with their children, disrespect and delinquency usually result. I remember a few years ago when my oldest son was a young teenager, he said to me, (after I had done something fatherly and cool), "You know what dad? You my dog, man". I knew what he meant but I did not want our relationship to diminish to a "home-boy" type relationship, so I responded by saying, "Son, I know what you mean but let's keep things clear - I am your dad, not your dog". I would never call my mother or father by their first name for that same reason. To this day, we have a respectable relationship and we are open to talk about everything.

The Bible has a lot to say about clearly defined home relationships, let's examine a few...

Ephesians 5:21-31, talks about the roles of husbands and wives toward each other and relates them to Christ and the church.

Ephesians 6:1-9, talks about the relationship dynamic between children and parents, servants and masters and relates both to Christ and the church.

And of course, Proverbs is filled with wisdom keys that start of with, "My Son...". Solomon sets a foundation of wisdom that will help anybody to handle proper family relationships and to walk honorably before other members of the family.

The concept of family transcends environment, ethnicity and event. This is God's design for your covering as you develop other relationships around you. This is why family has come under so much attack.

I strongly encourage everyone reading this book to strengthen your family relationship with everything you have. Pray for them and with them regularly, make phone calls, send cards and pictures. God designed the family as a covering to nurture, develop and reproduce "after its own kind".

Family is the solid core of every society on earth. The concept of family transcends environment, ethnicity and event. This is God's design for your covering as you develop more relationships around you. This is why family has come under so much attack. Efforts have been made to redefine family, marriage and the like. Ultimately, it is an attack God since family is an inspired relationship that represents His true nature in the world. It is human nature to attempt to redefine what you cannot control.

What we have to realize is that family is not just a name or title, it is dynamism. You can have a church family, corporate business family, or a sports family and still call a person brother or sister, because the dynamic is based upon the experiences that you share, and those experiences require a definition commensurate with the experiences you have shared.

Unfortunately, media has a lot to say about the definition of relationships in our society. A "friend" used to refer to a buddy, pal or girlfriend (female to female). In these days, a friend can refer to any of the above in addition to a sex partner, secret lover or sexual toy. Because we live in a post-modern society, many of the traditional definitions are passé and newly defined relationships are becoming part of our everyday lives. The definition of traditional marriage (between a man and a woman) is being challenged on every front. Television media is making a strong statement about relationships to youths that will have a long-term devastating effect on the future of America.

A "friend" used to refer to a buddy, pal or girlfriend (female to female). In these days, a friend can refer to any of the above in addition to a sex partner, secret lover or sexual toy.

As innocent and therapeutic as they may appear, programs like, *The Jerry Springer Show, Queer Eye for the Straight Guy and South Park* to name a few, use humor and chic to disguise the abnormalcy and perversion creeping into the minds of youths who watch television for hours at a time. The seduction through imagery is deadly because our youth are constantly bombarded by what Satan sinisterly wants to take away from the traditional family and the sting and the reality of sin and dysfunction by making it funny and cool and "not that big of a deal".

Humor has always been used as a means to anesthetize people from the pains of sin. Dysfunctional behavior seems to be the norm. Abusive relationships are now being unveiled and parent-child relationships have crossed virtually all previously defined lines of order.

Technology brings a SWF, 35, CP, 5'6", to a DHM, 42, CW. Translated, that means single white female, age 35, who is a Christian Protestant, height 5'6", to a Divorced Hispanic, Male, age 42 who loves Country/Western music. Internet dating is connecting people together at an unprecedented rate. Unfortunately, God's influence in establishing a mate divinely appointed to you is taken out of the formula. It will be interesting to see marital statistics on the outcome of these relationships in the future. My question is... What if a person's divinely orchestrated mate is not in their database?

There is a right way to date and a wrong way to date. There is a holy way and then there is a counterfeit way.

DATING RELATIONSHIPS

There is a right way to date and a wrong way to date. There is a holy way and then there is a counterfeit way. Here are some dating styles counterfeit unto the Lord that are all based on situational dynamics with unclear definitions and intentions. You may find these funny...

Discipleship Dating

This is when a person says, *"I am going to help that brother or sister grow in the Lord"*. They use discipleship as an opportunity to get isolated with a sister. Let me give you an example from my own story. When I first gave my life to Christ, long before I met my wife, I was dating a young lady in another church. She was pretty, voluptuous and knew less about God than I did. It was perfect! I decided to "witness" to her on an isolated part of a beach in Norfolk, Virginia. I brought the wine, bread and some music; she brought the blankets and made some sandwiches. Oh, I had my Bible too! It was a beautiful summer day. We decided to go swimming before we got into the Word. But when that girl took off her shirt to put on her bathing suit (Lord, have mercy!) ...discipleship time was over.

Many relationships end up on the chopping block because insecure people feed on the insecurities of others.

The problem with Discipleship Dating is that God's design for soul-winning should not be mixed with fleshly motives. Camouflaging the date is camouflaging the divine nature of the date.

Missionary Dating

This is when a person "reaches out" to the special needs of a person in the church as a sort of mission. The problem here occurs when, instead of leading the person to the Lord, you lead them elsewhere. Many relationships end up on the chopping block because insecure people feed on the insecurities of others. If a relationship is based on needs being met, either the needs will never get resolved or the relationship heads toward co-dependency, neither of which is healthy.

Video Dating

No, this not the internet relationship as you might suspect. This type of dating is about imagery. It says, "I am dating you because you look like the movie star that I fantasize about". This is dangerous because the attraction is fake and temporary. It is certainly not biblical. Usually one person does not know their appearance is the only thing that keeps the relationship going. Once the truth is revealed someone is going to be hurt.

Pharisee Dating

This type of dating implies doing what is right in public, but behind closed doors the dating aspect takes on a totally different behavior. Jesus exposed the Pharisees' deeds and called them, "*Whitewashed tombs*". They were super-righteous and held the society in bondage with religious rules and laws. Divine relationships are transparent and integritous. It is important to know that everything done in darkness shall be revealed in the light.

> *"And this is the condemnation, that light is come into the world of the world, and men loved darkness rather than light, because their deeds were evil. For everyone that doeth evil hateth the light, neither comes to the light, lest his deeds*

> *be reproved. But he that doeth truth cometh to the light, that his deeds may be manifest that they are wrought in God.*
>
> John 3:19-21

Stealth Dating

Stealth Dating goes for its kill at night. Did you notice that its root word is *steal*? Like the leopard, it strategically scopes out its prey over a period of time and then at the right moment, they exchange email addresses or phone numbers, business cards or offer an invitation to do lunch. This type of dating is particularly dangerous because it is so subtle and quick that even the most seasoned church mother could not detect that an illicit rendezvous ever occurred. After one party has attained their goal, they act like as though the relationship never took place.

We teach the Porter's Ministry (Mark 13:33,34) in our church, where we encourage and train the leadership and membership to watch and pray about what is really going on in and around the church. Senior leadership and staff are highly encouraged to watch – not judge, the sheep and the relationship dynamics. If you have enough conscientious porters in the church, many of the stealthy types will get exposed, and vulnerable women won't find themselves isolated with the "wolf spirit".

For a long time the subject of dating was taboo in the church. It seems that within the last 10-15 years the subject has come out of the wood work. Unfortunately, church leaders discovered that many of their young "church girls", were becoming pregnant and the young boys were becoming daddies before they learned adult level responsibilities. What we now know is what has been in front of our eyes all the long, which is that the same social challenges secular society faces, present themselves to the young within the church as well. "I Kissed Dating Goodbye" (2003), the very popular book was right in focusing the attention on serving God rather than the flesh. It works for some, but for the majority, teaching responsible dating practices may be a viable option as well. Let's face it, young people are going to be inquisitive about the opposite sex and the best thing we can do, is to prepare them by ensuring they know how to clearly define the relationships with whom they are connecting. Adults and teenagers need to see positive role models and be taught (in their language) the real truths about dating.

If a brother in the church is going to be a true brother or friend, it is important to keep the relationship clearly defined, otherwise, accountability plunges and compromising situations too often occur.

FOUR SEASONS OF MAN

I teach that there are four primary seasons of development in a person's life.

They are that of being a Son (or daughter), a brother (or sister), a husband (or wife) and then a father (or mother). The rules of engagement embracing the four seasons of a man (or woman) are simple:

1. Don't skip seasons
2. The seasons are not age specific
3. The character of the previous season will be with you always

The first season is to be a S**on** (or daughter). This season must be clearly defined and is vitally important to embrace. It is during this season of life that a person learns to receive instruction. They learn that there are consequences for negative and positive behaviors and to have plenty of room to enjoy life. During this stage, it is natural to be immature and silly! The blessing of being a son is that you have someone over you to call mom or dad and speak into your life. The desire to call upon a Father was supplied through Christ, when we accept His sacrifice. Oddly, regardless of age, people instinctively are looking for a father or mother figure in their lives, especially in the church.

Galatians 4:1 says,

> *...[That] the heir, as long as he is a child, differs nothing from a servant, though he be lord of all; but is under tutors* (to teach) *and governors* (to regulate) *until the time appointed of the father.*

When a person embraces this season, they naturally grow into the second season which is to be a brother or sister. Failure to fully embrace your "son" season usually results in not being adequately prepared to be a solid brother. It is here that you learn that there are consequences for positive and negative behaviors. Sons should be encouraged to enjoy the days of their youth, explore, dream and be adventurous. As these life experiences unfold, their rite of passage into the next stage can occur without warning and certain things will be said or actions done that let the parent know that the child's season is changing. Consider Jesus ....

Luke 2:40-52 says,

> *"And the child grew, and waxed strong in spirit, filled with wisdom: and the grace of God was upon Him". And it came to pass, that after three days they found him in the temple, sitting in the midst of doctors, both hearing them, and asking them questions. And all that heard him was astonished at his understanding and answers. And when they saw him, they were amazed: and his mother said unto him, Son, why hast thou dealt with us? Behold, thy father and I have sought thee sorrowing. And he said unto them, How is it that ye sought me? Wist ye not that I must be about my Father's business? And they*

> *understood not the saying which he spake unto them. And he went down with them, and came to Nazareth and was subject unto them; but his mother kept all these sayings in her heart."*

Mary knew what was going on. She knew that Jesus' season had changed, and the next time we hear from Jesus, He is a grown man being baptized by John the Baptist (Luke 3). My point here is that with the change of season, there is another re-definition of the relationship dynamic that is evident to those involved in the relationship.

Failure to fully embrace your season usually results in not being adequately prepared for being a solid brother.

I have several "**Daughters** in the faith" in my church. These young ladies vary in age and (interestingly) marital status. Some are very educated while others are not. The common denominator is that they all look toward me as their "Father in the Faith". Recently, one of them expressed her desire for a deepening relationship that went beyond church membership. She is from Nigeria and is a precious daughter, who calls me "Da-dee pastor", especially while she is away from her natural family in Africa.

As this father-daughter relationship developed, I noticed that she seemed to come alive spiritually. It is amazing to me to see her confidence emerge and their faithfulness increase simply because there is a father figure in her life. These daughters are open to receive correction, chastisement and constructive criticisms as necessary without fear of judgment or rejection. During this season, daughters learn to develop a sense of esteem and self-worth that will be with them for the rest of their lives. Thankfully, as children of God, we are given several changes to redeem the divine relationships regardless of age. So, if a young lady grows up without a father figure in her life, she has opportunity to embrace our heaven Father, who is a "Father to the fatherless". God has a way of telling them that they are appreciated for how special and precious and unique they truly are.

My wife teaches them to cook, walk by faith, and share stories with them to prepare them for their next season of life. Regardless of age or background, they embrace this time of impartation as valuable life lessons.

Brothers are born for adversity. During this season, you learn the lessons of accountability, responsibility and preparedness. Sons are prepared for manhood by learning to be accountable. The concept of teamwork and cooperation is introduced here. They learn the dynamics of family, friendship and leadership.

Genesis 4:9 asks the question,

> *"Where is your brother ...and he answered, Am I my brother's keeper?"*

My answer for my biological sons is ABSOLUTELY. One day, they will look back and laugh at how much trouble they got in and out of because they had each others back.

David and Jonathan's hearts "were knit together, they made a covenant because he loved him as his own soul; Jonathan stripped himself of his robe, and gave David his sword, his bow and his girdle" (I Sam 18). You don't normally do this as a child, but during this particular season you learn the importance of making sacrifices for someone else.

I have a precious friend who I consider to be a brother to me in Brooklyn named Cal Jones. We haven't seen each other in 25 years. Recently, my wife and I went to NYC for business and we finally got the opportunity to reconnect. It was wonderful! It was as if those years were immediately bridged and we picked up where we left off as teenagers. We met at a restaurant in Manhattan and reminisced about what we did as brothers in our group, *"The Jive Five"*, and laughed for hours until the restaurant closed. It is important to have brothers (or sisters) to share precious moments like these. If you have people in your life who are like a brother of sister to you, biologically or not.... cherish it. These types of relationships keep you grounded, humble and real.

Sisters need solid sisters in their lives to do the same. Some sisters are not afraid to get up close and personal and tell their sister-girlfriends how things really are without fear of repercussion.

As relationships develop, I teach that a strong-willed man needs a strong-willed woman and a strong-willed woman needs a secure, strong-willed man to balance out their lives. I do not recommend for strong willed women to be intimately involved with weak-willed men and vice-versa; it can breed co-dependency and infidelity and abuse; especially if there are plans for marriage and raising children.

How important is it, to have a sister in your life to confide in, trust and be "real" with, without having to be pretentious? When a true sister comes into your life, you have a valuable friend who can understand you and help you prepare for your next season of life which is that of being a wife.

Strong women do not need weak men in their lives; it can breed co-dependency and infidelity.

Many frustrated married partners are stuck in a relationship that is co-dependent instead of being inter-dependent. Instead of being married to a confident man, they realize that they are married to some woman's child.

The next season of a man is to be a **Husband**. The way a person handles conflict as a brother prepares them to resolve conflict as a husband. A successful marriage feeds on the willingness of each partner to support, honor and be honest with each other. If a person has not learned these lessons in the previous season, they may not be ready for marriage. Many marriage counselors will tell you that when a couple marries too early or without adequate life experience, there is a higher propensity for divorce, whether they are Christian or not. Husbands know that love means bonding with another imperfect person, just like themselves, to live in a perfect covenant established by God, called marriage. Without God, it will be difficult to honor your life partner because you have no basic foundation to understand personal flaws in character. Sociologists have known for years that couples fair better where they worship together, pray together and attend church together.

I teach that husbands need to know what "covering" is about, <u>before</u> becoming a father. When boys become fathers before their time, or when girls become mothers before their season, they run the risk of not being properly equipped with the knowledge of proper life lessons to instill integrity and how to maintain a secure, long term relationship.

Husbands have learned that brotherhood translates into being a peace maker and a protector for those who you love.

For women, becoming a **Wife** is a huge leap of faith. At this season of life you become an enhancer of the vision of the husband. You embrace companionship which involves creativity, resourcefulness and support. Wives have the unique responsibility of making a house, a home filled with love and warmth.

The Bible says in Proverbs 18:22, “Whoso findeth a wife findeth a good thing, and obtaineth favour of the LORD or as the Message Bible puts it, “Find a good spouse, you find a good life and even more: the favor of GOD!”. I recommend that before a couple decides to get married, they be good friends for a while. The longer, the better! This is because the authenticity developed as a brother or sister makes a smoother transition into holy matrimony.

When boys become fathers before their time, or when girls become mothers before their season, they run the risk of not being properly equipped with the knowledge of the life lessons to instill integrity and how to maintain a secure, long term relationship.

Being a **Father** is a very special season of life because as the progenitor, your seed is alive and looking at you in the face. It involves mentoring and you have to embrace being a role model. What we do now in moderation, the next generation will do in excess. Everything changes when you enter this season. For example, when a dad says', *Do as I say, not as I do*", or a mom says to her daughter, *"Don't grow up like I did"*, they are referencing a season of life that has missing pieces, but now that they are parents, they can only try to teach lessons that they themselves didn't take full advantage of during their youth.

I will discuss the "*Pata*" Blessing later in the book, but for now, suffice it to say that being a parent (or grand parent) is an honor because you take on the attributes that God would have over mankind. There are many blessings and rewards here that go beyond your own life. Honorable fathers know that there is a reflection of their lifestyle, words and actions to speak, breathe into and invest into others. It is a joy to see loved ones secure under the canopy of your protection and valuing the strength of your words.

Moms make the world go round. The dynamic of family rests in the lap of mothers who give birth, sacrifice and tolerate human imperfection to a depth that only another mother could understand. Throughout the scriptures, we find mothers who have gone through obstacles and challenges for their child, only to see them succeed or fail and in the end, it is the mother who is there embracing the child. Mothers are role models also. Ezekiel 16:44 says (regarding the children of Israel), "...everyone who makes up proverbs will say of you, 'like mother, like daughter'." Most people I know who have a well balanced life attribute their success to their mothers. Consider who athletes and celebrities acknowledge first when they receive an award or special recognition... their mom. I believe moms are a special gift of God to all of us, whether they are grand-moms, step-moms or play-moms, we all benefit from having a mom in our lives.

IN THE WORKPLACE

In the corporate world as well as in the church world, we are surrounded by people that challenge us, support us, stretch us and unfortunately, some frustrate us. Many times the reason for frustration is because the nature of the relationship is not clearly defined. Is it possible to have a divine (God inspired) relationship in the workplace? Absolutely! The nature of God supersedes the nature of man, His laws work regardless of your location or environment. As I mentioned previously, when a relationship is clearly defined, willingly embraced and freely invested in, it facilitates the environment for healthy relationships to continue. Any supervisor will confirm that when a faithful employee knows who they are in the workplace, they can have a healthy working relationship with others. They become team players and they are supportive of group goals. It would be no problem to send this type of employee to training conferences, or support them with the tools to get the job done the right way, because the nature of your relationship is right.

The ingredients for a divine relationship transcend the environment because they are based on principles of God.

I once had a young lady work in one of my departments tell me that she prayed for an opportunity to work on our team. She prayed for the favor of God during the interview. She asked God to send her to a Christian supervisor and co-workers. Because God honored her prayer, she obligated herself to do her part by, coming to work on time (if not early), doing her best every time and never spreading gossip or rumors. When I began to hear about her commitment to the department and her work ethic, it was easy to select her for some of the special projects I could delegate. This was a type of divine relationship based on loyalty, commitment and trust.

The ingredients for a divine relationship transcend the environment because they are based on principles of God. How many times has misjudging a work relationship gotten someone fired, sued or demoted?

Let me help you... Here are a few terms that exist in the workplace that often cause confusion.... acquaintance, colleague, protégé, mentor, associate, representative, supervisor, subordinate, co-worker and boss.

When these relationships are clearly defined verbally or non-verbally, written or unwritten, it sets boundaries that are conducive for a continuous healthy relationship to exist. There is safety here because when both parties continuously monitor the nature of their relationship. It keeps everyone involved balanced and reduces the temptation to cross the line.

Healthy relationships are reality-based. Healthy individuals don't deny emotions; ignore problems or tip-toe around "undiscussable" issues.

All expressions of flattery, gestures, gifts or flirtations should be viewed as appropriate or inappropriate as defined by the nature of the relationship. Many adulterous affairs are perpetuated in the workplace by people who are unable to maintain the boundaries of a professional relationship. They should allow it to naturally evolve to the next level as appropriate within the corporate structure.

Here are a few key ingredients to a healthy relationship:

1) Realism. Healthy relationships are reality-based. Healthy individuals don't deny emotions; ignore problems or tip-toe around "undiscussible" issues. Anytime parties involved in a relationship overlook the reality aspects of their relationship, they risk losing its authenticity and genuineness. As a result the relationship cannot withstand any challenges or tests.

2) Honesty. Healthy relationships cannot exist on a foundation of dishonesty. The more lies, denials, deception and secrets - the more dysfunctional the relationship becomes. Any couple, minister or supervisor who bases the relationship on dishonesty, gives room for the enemy of God to run amuck in the relationship. It is necessary to build any relationship on honesty in order for it to end in honesty. So if the relationship is for a reason or a season, the hurt that comes with the departure is not as great.

3) Vulnerability. The freedom to be vulnerable enables the relationship to grow. We need to know that we can disclose our deepest selves, our most intimate secrets our hurts, our dreams (without fear of being laughed at), our emotions - and that each and every secret will remain safe and secure within the enclosure of that relationship. The area

of vulnerability is associated with a level of trust beyond question. With God we should render ourselves vulnerable to receive guidance, correction and encouragement. If a couple endeavors to marry for instance, the man must be willing to pull down the wall that protects his ego and the woman must pull down the wall that guards her emotions and feelings.

4) Forgiveness. Every relationship has its share of hurts and disappointments. It is forgiveness that enables a relationship to survive the painful passages of life and allow it to grow and flourish. Forgiveness resolves the past and current issues and clears a path into the future for those involved. When you forgive someone, you not only set them free but you also free yourself. It takes a lot of energy to hold a grudge. I had a cousin who did not like me and I didn't like him either - even though we looked alike. When we were little boys he knocked over my bicycle and I kicked him and we got into a fight and I didn't tell anybody. That ended any friendship that could have developed. During family reunions, aunts and uncles would always try to get us together, and in my mind, there was no way! Then ten or fifteen years later at another family get together we met. I am still mad at him - and he at me - and we are avoiding one another like the plague. The problem now was that neither of us could

remember what we were mad about. Until my sister Rene reminded us that issue was over a bicycle. How silly! Don't laugh; you probably have it in your family too!

5) Security. A healthy relationship is a secure harbor in an uncertain world. Everyone needs a relationship that goes beyond "pleasantries" and has the depth to withstand the pressures that challenges its existence and purpose. The key to true security in a relationship is in the trust and confidence of those involved. There can be no fear or insecurity in any way, shape or form or else the security of the relationship is in jeopardy. 1 John 4:18 has an answer for us,

"*There is no fear in love, but perfect love casts out fear.*"

As each relationship undergoes change and transition, there is no room for fear. Fear, doubt and unbelief in a relationship are like cancer to the body.

6) Trust. Once trust is lost, it is difficult to get it back. This is because it requires the giving of oneself almost to the point of dependency. Many adults who once trusted people who they thought knew how of handle confidentiality, find themselves at a loss because their ability to trust people is gone. Unfortunately,

this inability to trust again, spills over into so many other areas that if it is not restored, the person will become critical and isolated and will not know how to enjoy gifts, love or how to confide in others.

This is dangerous because we were not created to be isolated from others. We were created to be socially interactive beings and we cannot grow in isolation. Those who try to live in isolation are attempting to violate the basic nature that was designed for us during Creation (See Genesis 2:18).

7) Sacrifice. Lastly, it is impossible to have a healthy relationship without sacrifice. It means being willing to give up some of our rights during times of conflict. This will help every couple settle arguments, parents to settle disputes with their children and workers to understand their bosses better. Dads must know and embrace their responsibilities as a priest in their family. There are two excellent examples in Hebrews, one referring to Moses, "*...Choosing rather to suffer affliction with the people of God, than to enjoy the pleasures of sin for a season*" (Hebrews 11:25); and the second referring to Jesus in Hebrews 7:22-27.

"By so much was Jesus made a surety of a better covenant. Also they truly were priests, because they were suffered to continue by reason of death.

But He (Jesus), because He continues forever, has an unchangeable priesthood. Therefore He is also able to save to the uttermost those who come to God through Him, since He always lives to make intercession for them. For such a High Priest was fitting for us, who is holy, harmless, undefiled, separated from sinners, and has become higher than the heavens; who does not need daily, as those high priests, to offer up sacrifices, first for He did once for all when He offered up Himself."

Jesus is a perfect example of what sacrifice in a relationship entails. In this passage of scripture, the writer shows Jesus as being holy, harmless, undefiled and separated from sinners, one who doesn't need daily sacrifices because He offered up Himself as a sacrifice for everyone. When those involved in a divine relationship are willing to make sacrifices, that is, to give up of themselves and become holy, harmless, undefiled and separated from sin, there is no room for abuse, infidelity, and neglect.

The revelation is that Jesus Christ is more than a prophet, more than a teacher, He is the Christ - The Son of the Living God and your relationship with the Father comes only through His Son. John 14:6 says,

"I am the way, the truth, and the life: no man cometh unto the Father but by me".

By now, you should begin to take a closer examination at the relationships surrounding your life. Go ahead, ask yourself, "Why is this person in my life at this time?" "Can I clearly define it without any alteration?" "Are they a friend or foe, asset or liability, to strengthen or to weaken, to compliment or complicate my life?"

These very important questions lead to our next phase - to Willingly Embrace what has been previously defined.

LET'S PRAY

Heavenly Father... I thank you for the people who have divinely placed in my life. I pray that who would help me to cherish and honor those who have helped me and encouraged me along the way; and forgive me for neglecting those who I should have paid more respect to. I am discovering that you have been with me all the long and now know the importance of clearly defining the relationships in and around my life.

Thank you for your good hand that is upon my life.

In Jesus' name.
Amen.

PRINCIPLES TO LIVE BY

- Misjudging the nature of any relationship can lead you to be frustrated, misunderstood, hurt, angry or disappointed.

- Most people I know who are doing well in ministry, marriage or career have a continual openness in expressing the nature of their relationship with others.

- When relationships are clearly defined verbally or non-verbally, written or unwritten, it sets boundaries that are conducive for a continuous healthy relationship to exist.

- Every Christian needs a covering - someone who they trust, but who will also teach, correct, guide, protect and feed with knowledge and understanding.

- I believe that God does not want to have a platonic or distant relationship with man. He does not want to be professional with you or be your colleague. **We are not at His level.**

- When parents don't clearly define the relationship with their children disrespect and delinquency usually result.

Section 2

Every Healthy Relationship Must Be...

Willingly Embraced

John 15:4
"Abide in me, and I in you. As the branch cannot bear fruit of itself, except it abide in the vine; no more can ye, except ye abide in me."

Once the purpose of a relationship has been clearly defined, the next step is to Willingly Embrace the relationship - not grudgingly but willingly. The Father has designed our success and prosperity according to our ability to embrace His Will. The more we embrace Him, trust Him and agree with Him, the more He proves Himself strong on our behalf. This chapter will deal a Genesis principle I call, "the Principle **of Agreement**," how to overcome offenses and key roles men and women play in the family.

I will go out on a limb here by saying, when a person says "No" to God, they limit their effectiveness as a leader and they disqualify themselves of being blessed by Him". I believe firmly that people who are blessed by the Lord don't tell God, "No". They have somehow tapped into the profound truth that God has a plan charged with prosperity for our lives; all we have to do is say, "Yes, Lord", and agree with Him and wonderful things will begin to happen.

Saying "No", to God will limit your effectiveness as a leader and will cut off your availability to be blessed by Him.

The Principle of Agreement says, "Yes Lord", even if I don't understand it all or have all the answers. This Genesis Principle is so profound that even God Himself has to operate by it – because He created (Hebrew:

Bara) it. And by it created He the world and blessed it (*Barak*). Genesis 1:26 says,

> *"Let us make man in our image, and after our likeness: and let them have dominion..."*

In other words, before He could create anything He has to agree with Himself to do it. Similarly, in order for a person to Willingly Embrace the relationship, they have to agree with the definition as stated in the previous chapter. The Principle of Agreement is a universal principle that transcends the church and is valid in every aspect of our lives (just like Seed Time and Harvest, The Law of Exchange, and Sowing and Reaping). Your marriage, money and your ministry are governed by this simple principle; and it holds its own in the natural as well as in the supernatural. It works whether you are born again or not.

Consider this... Faith at its essence is based on the principle of Agreeing with God on matters that you cannot see with the natural eye, but on what God says spoken.

Here are a few points I teach in my church regarding the Principle of Agreement.

- Agreement shifts the power and changes the atmosphere
- You can change the **atmosphere** in your home, church and city by what you agree with in the spirit.

- When you set the atmosphere, you set the **climate** (conditions for angels to be released and miracles to occur)
- When you set the climate, you establish the **culture** (condition of the people) for the miracles to occur.
- Agreement sets the atmosphere for FAITH and MATURITY to be released

THREE THINGS THAT AGREEMENT PRODUCES:

1. PRODUCES POWER (Matthew 18:18-*20) My Spirit agrees with the Word of God, My Soul agrees with my Spirit, My Flesh agrees with my Soul,

- There is a (confirming and demonstrative) witness where there is agreement.
- Matthew 3:17 ("...This is my beloved Son, in whom I am well pleased.")
- I John 5:7 (..."there are three that bear record in Heaven: The Father, Word, and the Holy Ghost...")
- I John 5:8 ("...there are three that bear witness in the earth, the Spirit, and the water, and the blood: and these three agree in one.")
- ***Acts 2:1 ("...they were all with one accord in one place. **And suddenly**...")

2. FACILITATES PROGRESS Amos 3:3 says, *How can two walk together unless they agree*?

The "walking" here is synonymous with progress. Everything that is alive operates on the Principle of Agreement.

You cannot force someone to love you, nor should you coerce someone to be your friend.

Relationships grow, mature and develop according to the faith released in agreement. Plants will grow faster and stronger when there is an agreement of the conditions (sunlight, water, fertilized soil). People are the same way. When a person clearly defines a relationship and willingly embraces its definition, the responsible thing to do is to simply agree, even if it hurts a little. If a person is unwilling to receive that definition, someone is going to be frustrated and deeper hurt is inevitable. You cannot force someone to love you, nor should you coerce someone to be your friend. What many do not realize is that God has a way of turning things around. The miraculous is put on hold until acceptance of the definition is established.

Here's another Biblical example. Matthew 9:28 (MSG) says,

> *"And when He (Jesus) was come into the house, the blind men came to him: and Jesus saith unto them, Believe ye that I am able to do this? They said unto him, Yea, Lord. And He touched their*

> *eyes and said, "**Become what you believe**.*" (emphasis added)

Every miracle Jesus performed was precipitated by a point of agreement. As a matter of fact, before I can progress toward accomplishing my goals, I have to agree with myself that I will do such and such a thing. This is where self-conflict or inner-conflict emerges. When a person is in conflict with themselves, there is a great chance that they will not accomplish any given goal. These goals can range from completing an application to deciding whether or not to get involved in a relationship.

3. <u>CHANGES THE ATMOSPHERE</u>

Albert Einstein once said, *"The significant problems we face cannot be solved from the same level that we created them, we must go up – in order to solve our problems"*

In Mark 9:14-29, we see another miracle performed by the Master. The miracle was preceded by the Principle of Agreement, which shifted the power from Christ's ability to heal to the man's faith to believe. Once the atmosphere is set and faith is released, the climate (the environment of the group) is shifted toward the whole culture and the pervading character of the whole environment is shifted to believe God. For instance, when the Word of Faith is spoken in the midst of a group of believers, it stirs up the faith of everyone in the room. Now, what was originally given for one person can now be embraced by everyone and the pervading character of the whole environment is shifted to that Word.

Faith, at its essence, is based on the Principle of Agreeing with God on matters that we cannot see with the natural eye, and what God has spoken. You cannot walk in faith without walking in agreement with God's Word.

> (v24) *"The father of the child cried out, and said with tears, Lord I believe; help thou mine unbelief."*

What was he saying? I believe he places a touch of realism to the situation. He is saying, "There are things I can believe God for, and there are things I need help in believing God for, help thou mine unbelief".

Isn't it interesting that many miracles in the Bible occur when man's resources and abilities have been exhausted? For some, we can have the faith for easy things like a parking space at the mall, or healing for someone else, but when it comes to the larger things like reconciliation or making the next electric bill payment, we pray, *"Lord, help thou mine unbelief."* This is where miracles occur; not when you want one, but when you need one! They come when you align yourself in agreement with what God has to say about those things that are beyond your control, resources and ability.

I will go out on another limb by saying this: saying "No", in the establishment or development of any relationship, redefines it and can lead to a premature end. In 1 Peter 2:8, 9 we find these words,

> "*You used to be disobedient, but now you are a chosen generation (which speaks to your place in history), a royal priesthood (which speaks to your position in God) a holy nation (which speaks to your place in the world), and a peculiar people (which speaks to your place among other people), that you should show forth the praises of Him who hath called you out of darkness and into His marvelous light*".

During our dating phase, when the time came to take the relationship between my wife and I to its next level, I had to ask her key questions. If answered correctly it would determine if we could go to the next level. If they were not, I would have to make a decision. As things got more serious, I had to break out my "checklist" to see if she "qualified" to be my wife. Little did I know that she had a checklist of her own.

The ultimate question was of course... "Will you marry me?" But before I asked that question, I had to know...

1. Can she cook from scratch?
2. Does she have the right goals and dreams?

3. Is she high maintenance or naturally economical?
4. Is she a chicken and afraid of heights (because I knew that living with me would be the roller coaster ride of a lifetime)?

Don't laugh. Your list is probably stranger than mine! (The above, is a brief sample of a much more extensive list, for an excellent example, I recommend the book, *"Single Wisdom: Empowering Singles, Divorcees, Widows & Widowers for Living"* by Dr. Paris Finner-Williams, where she provides a 150 point screening questionnaire and a 6 month evaluation for future spouse selection. She even recommends getting criminal and financial background checks and character references <u>before</u> getting married. (*Yes! it is that important).*

Nevertheless her answer had to be "Yes", to all of the above; otherwise our relationship could not advance. In other words, she had to willingly embrace my proposal, before I could make an appropriate investment.

There are a few key scriptural examples that depict what I call "Defining Moments", which set in motion a series of events that could change a person's life forever.

What would have happened if Moses had said, "No", to the call to confront Pharaoh in letting God's people go? Or, if Joseph (Gen. 3) would have refused those dreams of destiny that were much larger than he expected. He, like us, had to respond in a manner that allowed God to set in motion key events that would make his dreams become a reality and eventually save His people. There are so many Biblical stories to choose from, all you would have to do is to closely examine any major Biblical character, and you will begin to see the pattern that led to the purpose for writing this book.

I teach that there are **four types of witnesses** given to help us embrace things that God is trying to tell us. They are the Intuitive Witness, the Audible Witness, the Confirming Witness and the Demonstrative Witness

1. **The Intuitive (or Internal) Witness**. This is your inner voice or the voice of your conscience. It is usually still and small. You will hear this voice when God initially speaks into your life. If not acted upon right then, the voice will go dormant until God begins to speak audibly to you. Many times God births a Word of destiny into us as children. They are expressed as future goals and aspirations to become a pilot, CEO or school teacher. Some children are so open to receive God's intuitive voice, that they actually speak it out and parents will surround them (to the best of their ability and resources) to ensure that it happens. The seed of destiny can be so deeply planted in their young lives that regardless of the life experiences they encounter as teenagers and young adults – it

never leaves them. Every time they touch something related to their destiny, their spirit will be stirred. It is here that the wooing of the Holy Spirit begins to guide you as to what to say, what to do or who to allow into your life.

2. **The Audible Witness**. The second witness is the one where God speaks and you hear it but no one else might. In 1 Samuel 3:4-12 (NIV), the young Samuel hears a voice in the middle of the night calling his name. He goes into the room of his mentor, the Prophet Eli ...

> *"One night Eli, whose eyes were becoming so weak that he could barely see, was lying down in his usual place. The lamp of God had not yet gone out, and Samuel was lying down in the temple of the LORD, where the ark of God was. Then the LORD called Samuel. Samuel answered, "Here I am." And he ran to Eli and said, "Here I am; you called me."* ***But Eli said, "I did not call; go back and lie down."*** *So he went and lay down. Again the LORD called, "Samuel!" And Samuel got up and went to Eli and said, "Here I am; you called me." "My son," Eli said, "I did not call; go back and lie down." Now Samuel did not yet know the LORD: The word of the LORD had not yet been revealed to him. The LORD called Samuel a third time, and Samuel got up and went to Eli and said, "Here I am; you called me." Then Eli realized that the LORD was calling the boy. So Eli told*

> *Samuel, "Go and lie down, and if he calls you, say, 'Speak, LORD, for your servant is listening.' So Samuel went and lay down in his place. The LORD came and stood there, calling as at the other times, "Samuel! Samuel!" Then Samuel said, "Speak, for your servant is listening." And the LORD said to Samuel: "See, I am about to do something in Israel that will make the ears of everyone who hears of it tingle."* (emphasis added)

A similar thing happened to the Apostle Paul while he was on his way to Damascus in Acts 9:1-5 (MSG).

> *"When he got to the outskirts of Damascus, he was suddenly dazed by a blinding flash of light. As he fell to the ground, he heard a voice: "Saul, Saul, why are you out to get me?" He said, "Who are you, Master?" "I am Jesus, the One you're hunting down. I want you to get up and enter the city. In the city you'll be told what to do next."* ***His companions stood there dumbstruck—they could hear the sound, but couldn't see anyone****—while Saul, picking himself up off the ground, found himself stone-blind. They had to take him by the hand and lead him into Damascus. He continued blind for three days. He ate nothing, drank nothing."* (emphasis added)

In both cases the Lord spoke audibly to the person in a way as to get their attention. He had something to say that would directly affect the lives of many other people living in that area. God will do the same for you. He will speak directly to you through dreams, visions or even angelic visitations that you cannot deny. Others may be around you at the time but they may not see or hear what you have heard or seen. The reality is that you will know that it happened and the lives of others hang in the balance.

3. **The Confirming Witness**. This is where someone else confirms or affirms what is happening in your life. You may not have to say anything to anyone, but the fruit of what has been spoken to you is clearly seen and expressed through others.

> "*The very next day John saw Jesus coming toward him and yelled out, "Here he is, God's Passover Lamb! He forgives the sins of the world! This is the man I've been talking about, 'the One who comes after me but is really ahead of me.' I knew nothing about who he was—only this: that my task has been to get Israel ready to recognize him as the God-Revealer*".
>
> John 1:29, 30 (MSG)

It is important to understand God's purpose for doing things this way. Sometimes the divine truths He will speak to you or insights He will give you are overwhelming; if you were to go out immediately and tell people what you heard or what you've seen, people may not take you seriously. But if people who really know you can confirm that truth or can witness what you are saying, you now have validity and credibility working on your side.

4. **The Demonstrative Witness**. This is the witness that demonstrates what has been previously stated. It cannot be denied, it cannot be stopped and things previously not understood, will be clearly understood.

> *"They sent them out of the room so they could work out a plan. They talked it over: "What can we do with these men? By now it's known all over town that a miracle has occurred, and that they are behind it. There is no way we can refute that."*
>
> Acts 4:15, 16 (MSG)

The background on this story is that Peter and John were thrown in jail for healing a man and preaching the Gospel of Jesus Christ where five thousand people became believers. The next day miraculously, they were back on the streets preaching. It was undeniable that God was working through their lives, not just for their sake, but for the sake of those who lived in that area. The Bible says,

> *"These miraculous signs will accompany those who believe: They will cast out*

> *demons in my name, and they will speak in new languages. They will be able to handle snakes with safety, and if they drink anything poisonous, it won't hurt them. They will be able to place their hands on the sick, and they will be healed. When the Lord Jesus had finished talking with them, he was taken up into heaven and sat down in the place of honor at God's right hand. And the disciples went everywhere and preached, and the Lord worked through them, confirming what they said by many miraculous signs.*
>
> Mark 16:17-20 (NLT)

It is important to know that these four witnesses work sequentially. In terms of relationships, God speaks to us internally about people and situations; some call it intuition, some call it a "gut feeling", regardless of what you call it, it is God's way of letting you know He is speaking.

Everyone may not hear what you are hearing or see what you are seeing, but you cannot deny what is real in your heart. When people confirm what they see in you, it is to give you confidence to make a move on what you may have been too intimidated to embrace previously. The demonstrative witness is so profound because once the manifestation or fruit of what was spoken to you in private becomes openly evident to others, you can expect your life to change.

This is true in the life of a young girl from Galilee named Mary.

A GIRL NAMED MARY

One of my favorite examples is the encounter young Mary had with the angel announcing that she would conceive a child (Luke 2). This is not just a Christmas story. It is our story! In Luke 1:28, the angel greets her by saying, "Hail, (1) Thou art highly favored, (2) The Lord is with thee, (3) Blessed art thou among women.

> (v29) *"And when she saw him she was troubled at his saying, and cast in her mind what manner of salutation this should be. And before she could say anything to talk her way out of this moment, the angel says (v30) Fear not, Mary: for thou hast found favor with God."*

The reason I say this story is not just a Christmas story is purely hermeneutical. I believe she had not been greeted like that very often. She was a poor girl, from the "not so good part of town", and she is in love with and just married a young man who does not have a lot to offer her. I wonder if Mary knew that she was highly favored of God <u>before</u> the angel visited her.

FOUR THINGS THE ANGEL SAID TO MARY
(and will say to us!) Luke 2:28-30

1. Thou art highly favored of God (even if you don't feel like it).
2. The Lord is with thee (even if it doesn't seem like it).
3. You are blessed among women (even though your conditions don't appear that way).
4. Fear not (even though you have no idea of the magnitude of what is about to happen in your life).

The first obstacle was overcoming fear and doubt. God was not going to allow fear – whether it is fear of success, her past, or what the townspeople would think of her - to preempt His plan for the redemption of mankind.

FOUR THINGS MARY SAID BACK TO THE ANGEL
(Luke 2:34, 38, 46)

1. How can this be? This is the typical response when God drops a kingdom dynamic in your heart. The answer however will always be the same – THE HOLY GHOST. It is here where she contends with the will to embrace something greater than herself.

2. Behold, the handmaid of the Lord. I believe Mary is starting to catch a hold of the fact that God can and will make a miracle of her mess! I can imagine her saying to herself, "I don't know how I'm going to explain this to Joseph but... with God nothing shall be impossible (v37), so let's do it! Here she is putting herself in a position to be blessed.

3. **Be it unto me according to thy Word**. Praise God, she got it! She embraces God's will for her life. This was the statement that sent the angel back to Heaven. Mission accomplished! When Mary got in faith to agree, even though she had no way of knowing how this would unfold in her life, she set in motion a divine relationship that would cause her name to be remembered every time the gospel is preached.

This same type of dynamic will happen to every person who reads this book. God will select you, and before He tells you what He is going to do in your life, tells you what you mean to Him, will comfort you with an understanding that says, "I am with you", and that you are blessed among women. All this, <u>before</u> He tells you what He is going to tell you, so you don't disqualify yourself because of your past life experiences and defeatism.

See, some of people have to be convinced that God can use them even with their faults, flaws, insecurities and bad habits. Notice that He didn't give her a chance to speak, before He said, "Fear not". He knew that she would respond in fear and talk herself right out of her divine destiny, just like many of us would do.

When Mary said, *"Be it unto me according to thy Word"*, (v38) she is uttering the same words God longs for us to say when He wants us to respond to Him!

It takes faith to willingly embrace such an invitation because many times it is too profound for what we experience in everyday living. There are times when God will speak to you with such clarity and vision for something that it may startle you, but the witness to do what He has shown you has to be confirmed through others.

After Mary accepts what is about to happen in her life, she goes to her pregnant cousin Elizabeth's house.

> *"And it came to pass, that when Elizabeth heard the salutation of Mary, the babe leaped in her womb and Elizabeth was filled with the Holy Ghost and said," Blessed art thou among women, and blessed is the fruit of thy womb."* (v45) *And blessed is she that believed: for there shall be a performance of those things which were told her from the Lord".*
>
> Luke 1:39-42

I believe that Elizabeth is the confirming witness to encourage Mary that another Divine Relationship is about to be birthed. Notice that Elizabeth used almost the exact wording that the angel used (compare v28 and v42). With each confirmation, it becomes a little easier to accept challenges and relationships with God and others that would otherwise be difficult to embrace.

4. My soul does magnify the Lord, and my spirit hath rejoiced in God my Savior.

> *"For He has regarded the low estate of His handmaiden for, behold, for behold, from henceforth all generations shall call me blessed."*
>
> Luke 1:46, 47

Not a bad statement for a young, poor girl from the impoverished side of town. This is where the manifestation or the demonstration of what she received is being boldly proclaimed. The rest of her story is known to everyone. She conceived a son, named Him Jesus and even to this day, her story is as popular as any other story in the entire Bible and has been told to children from generation to generation in practically every language on the planet.

MY TESTIMONY

Let me give you another example regarding my wife and me. While in the process of looking for a wife, I would bring potential candidates to church hoping the *Shekinah* glory would surround the "right one' and the Father would speak from Heaven and say, "This is The One, Marry Her!", like

He did with Jesus when He came out of water after being baptized by John the Baptist. Back then we had a Church Mother named Mother Rosa Garrett. Each time I brought a different young lady to church, Mother Garrett would look at me all the way from the opposite side of the church, and shake her head with displeasure. This went on for about three or four months. Once, I went to pick up one young lady and because we were running late, I did not thoroughly check what she was wearing. You must know that in our small Pentecostal, COGIC church, sanctified dress was the standard for everyone.

Well, when this young lady took off her coat, it was like she was dressed for the club, wearing a low-cut, very revealing and form fitting dress. I figured that I could smooth things over, as long as Mother Garrett didn't see her. I made sure we sat in the back, as far away from her as possible. My goal was to not make eye contact with Mother because I knew she would give me "The look", followed by "The head shake of rejection". Then, as the anointing filled the room, the preacher made a point, and everyone stood up to shout, "Amen", and Praise the Lord… except Mother Garrett. Her timing was impeccably perfect, as soon as I went to sit down, I glanced in her direction. Big mistake!

She looked at me and shook her head again with displeasure; I was humiliated. After church, I did my absolute best to avoid her because I knew that my friend was dressed like a Jezebel (that's what they called it back then). We almost made it to the car, when out of no where, 90 year old Mother Garrett appeared. She didn't even acknowledge my guest, but spoke directly to me. She said, "Sweets, I have something for you, come see me later on". Talk about conviction! Later that evening I visited with her briefly before the Sunday evening service started and we began to talk.

She gave me two pages of scriptures to read and a note at the bottom which read, "*A man will search the whole world for a treasure, only to find it at home*". To make a long story short, I went to NYC to visit my mother for Mother's Day. As some of my friends and I were dripping in sweat from playing basketball, there appeared my angel from out of no where, wearing jeans, a sweatshirt and walking her cocker spaniel. I rushed down to re-acquaint myself with her, and she brushed me off like I was some thuggish ghetto boy. After a few days we talked, laughed and shared how important it was to get out of Brownsville, before you got caught in the vacuum of underachievement. I told her I was stationed in Virginia, and ironically, she was moving to Virginia to begin her Master's degree work at Old Dominion University, ironically only 30 minutes away from where I lived. After she got settled in school, the day came when I invited her to my church. I checked what she was wearing and made her change clothes twice. She didn't understand that this was for her own good!

We arrived a little late so we had to sit toward the back of the church, fortunately, away from Mother Garrett who was always, second row, first seat on the left.

When the service ended I made a dash for the car but the pastor signaled me to come to him for some reason and Mother Garrett made her move. She walked right past me and went straight to Gwen and introduced herself. The pressure was on because I couldn't take the look nor the head shake at this point. Then with a smile she turned and winked her eye, "That's the one Sweets".

"How do you know, Mother?" I asked.

"Baby, within six months, you gonna marry that girl", and she hobbled away supported by her walking cane and humming a song. How prophetic her words were as in December of that year we were married.

My point in telling this story is that I had to embrace the word that came from Mother Garrett in order for my destiny to become a reality. Shortly after we were married, Mother Garrett went home to be with the Lord.

Let's examine the pragmatics of how the Principle of Agreement applies at church, home and at work.

IN THE CHURCH

When a person receives salvation through Jesus Christ, what he is actually doing is submitting himself to His Lordship. They position themselves to willingly embrace His grace, forgiveness and mercy, and in turn, God willingly embraces their nothingness and gives them a brand new life. What if God were to say, "I'm not going to receive you"; the plan of salvation would be halted. He would have to contradict His own plan, character and nature to do that. John 6:37 says,

> *"All that the Father giveth me shall come to me; and him that cometh to me I will in no wise cast out."*

Praise God that His nature and character is to embrace us, and look beyond our faults and see our needs. Truly, His grace is amazing!

Through prayer, we learn to talk to God and listen to what He says.

When people join the membership of a church, in order for them to develop into maturing Christians, three key behaviors must be embraced: consistent prayer, consistent attendance in Bible Study and consistent servitude. The idea of growing up spiritually without these three key behaviors is like arrested development- the potential is there but the result is disappointing. Through these, a person demonstrates their willingness to embrace God's ways, laws and gain knowledge as to the working of the Holy Spirit.

The analogy I often use is that of an equilateral triangle, or three-legged stool. When any one of the three is not engaged, a person's Christian life becomes out of balance. Through prayer, we learn to talk to God and listen to what He says. Prayer is the language of the kingdom, its how we communicate with our heavenly Father. In turn, He reveals His plans for our lives and gives us a glimpse of our destiny (see Jeremiah 29:11). He gives answers to the unsolvable and peace for the things we cannot control – we turn things over to Him and because He is a loving, caring and sharing heavenly Father, who shows Himself strong on our behalf.

Bible study gives us not only knowledge, but the opportunity to receive (embrace) concepts, truths and ideas that we may not understand on our own. It is easy to puff to myself up with my own understanding and become a legend in my own mind. The challenge is to embrace those things that are too high for us; things in the Bible we did not see or understand. You will know when a Bible Study session is good when you look at the faces of God's people and you can see the wonderment and awe of someone who expresses, "I never saw that before!" I love explaining Biblical concepts to students of the Word because when a revelation of truth is caught and embraced, it changes a person's life. When people miss Bible Study their development is hindered. I preach on Sunday's so that they may believe, I teach on Wednesday so that they may understand.

James 2:17-20 says,

> "*Even so faith, if it hath not works, is dead, being alone. Yes, a man may say, Thou hast faith and I have works: show me thy faith without thy works, and I will show thee my faith by my works.*"

Faith and works fit together like a hand in a glove, they are inseparable. Serving proves what you believe. Nothing validates your level of faith like serving. I will go out on a limb here and say that your prayer life and biblical knowledge are limited by what you do with the knowledge you have already received. Prayer tugs the heart of God to empower you to do what you normally do not have the strength, resources or connections to do on your own.

The challenges we face on a daily basis are just opportunities to exercise the things we have received through God's Word.

Here are some ways to relate the different levels of relationships within the church and how they are assimilated into the life of a believer.

Level	Definition	Assimilation
Membership	Deals with Identification	This is My church
Discipleship	Deals with Education	I can be taught here
Fellowship	Deals with Unification	I am connected here
Stewardship	Deals with Investment	I can sow into this ministry
Sonship	Deals with Inheritance	I have relationship here
Lordship	Deals with Submission	* This is our goal. Yes, Lord to your Will, Way and Word.

Have you noticed that in many contemporary, seeker-sensitive churches that the pastor is called by their first name, "Pastor Bob" or "Brother Bob"? The church has never been designed to be a social entity; we are a force to be reckoned with to deal with spiritual needs of people. The disciples referred to Jesus as, "Master", Lord" or Messiah"; I cannot find a scripture where any of them called Him, "Jesus". Even though I am sure they knew His first name, they willingly embraced His Lordship and would not disrespect Him by calling Him "Jesus". This is why children should never call their parents by their first name, but rather be trained to honor their parents, with "Mom",

"Dad" etc., God ordained hierarchy is respectable and honorable (see Ephesians 6:1,2)

ON THE HOMEFRONT

When families willingly embrace their roles and responsibilities, there is peace in the home. Recently, at one of our couples retreats, my wife and I ministered a simple chart that lays out some of the key roles and responsibilities between husbands and wives. What we have discovered over the years is that where these roles are missing, are the very areas where the enemy seeks to wreak havoc.

HUSBAND ROLES	WIVES ROLES
Priesthood The Priest must pray in the home. You become intimate with the one you pray with and the one you pray for. When a husband prays with and for his family he becomes intimate with them.	**Enhancer** The Enhancer shares the vision of her husband and works with him to accomplish what they were both created to do for the family. She is confident and trust-worthy and takes whatever the husband has provided and enlarges or extends it
Prophet (Prov 29:18) The prophet speaks and sees what God is showing him for the family. Vision sets goals which motivate a plan of action. It gives the family a reason to follow	**Companion** (Gen 2:18) This role describes the wife who helps share the load. A wife was probably a very good friend to her husband before they married. Her purpose and resourcefulness can be

or pursue a healthy family life. Pray the vision, talk the vision, walk the vision, rejoice in the vision and stay with the vision.

Peacemaker (Matt 5:5)
Blessed are the peacemakers. The peacemakers are quick to seek peace and closure because he knows that discontent distorts the vision. He will apologize for mistakes, misunderstanding and miscommunique (even if it is not their fault). Peacemakers destroy the yoke of silence by making peace the priority. Pride, ego and machoism are not honored when you allow hurt to continue to fester.

Provider (I Tim 5:8)
Providers make the investment in their family and themselves. The glory of a man is to give, build and maintain. They know that when you stop investing in yourself, you stop investing in your family.

Positive Role Model (Ex 18:19)
The best example of

the greatest asset a man has, beside himself. The term, "Life Partner" describes the role of the companion – they need each other.

Reflector (Eph 5:25, 28)
The reflector wife is the object of her husband's love and she reflects the love he gives her. When a wife receives love from her husband (spiritually and physically) she comes alive! When she doesn't she is like a short-circuited wire, no joy, no exuberance and no glow; she is just heavily burdened because she has nothing to reflect.

Life Giver (Gen 3:20)
Eve in the Hebrew language is *Chavvah*, which means "life-giver". She was given the ability to receive seed and reproduce after their kind. Her entire being is focused on creating life (children, finances, vision, even an idea). She multiplies what she is given, she is a walking, talking womb, and she conceives something... look out!

Leader (Ex 18:19,20)
It is commonly stated, "The hand that rocks the

godliness is to be an example of godliness. Show the family standards, order and holiness through patience, love and understanding. Teach the family integrity and the right way to do things as shown to you by God and His Word. They know to look to Jesus as the perfect role model.

cradle rules the world". The influence of a wife or mother is powerful; she has position-power and influence –power. This can be threatening to an insecure dad or husband. She has to be strong, courageous and gorgeous at the same time!

When these roles (and there are several more) are clearly defined and willingly embraced, there is little room for divorce, separation and adultery. One reason why Role Conflict occurs in the family is because wives and mothers are trying to do what the father or husband was designed to do. When men are out of their place, women instinctively try to compensate by trying to teach boys to become men and fix things on their own. With more women entering into the workforce, and the increase of male homosexuality and incarceration, roles are being reversed and conflict results. There are many boys that still need fathering, by godly men who are not biologically theirs. How many frustrated women do you know that are disappointed with the lack in number of "eligible" men with whom they can spend the rest of their lives with in joy and prosperity? They have so much to offer, but without a godly man to share it, the above attributes go dormant.

This is one reason why many women choose lesbianism as a lifestyle, because of compromise and the drama of dealing with a man who does not know his purpose.

The same is true for many men who have a long "qualification list" for a female to speak into, provide for and protect. The challenge of dealing with a "high maintenance" female is too dramatic, so a compromise is resultant. I believe this is one reason why pornography and masturbation is on the rise. Many men simply cannot find someone to share their lives with, so they "sow their oats" in the privacy of their closet.

IN THE WORKPLACE

When I was in the military, there were fraternization rules and regulations that were strictly enforced by senior officers and enlisted members. As a youngster, I did not understand the reasoning. To me, people were people - they just had more rank than I did. But that did not make them better than me, nor did it prevent me from doing my job. As I matured, I came to the realization that those rules were not just for peacetime but for wartime (as it was explained to me in no uncertain terms). During times of battle, your response should be, "Yes, Sir or Yes, Ma'am", to those who were in authority over you. So if or when your commander says, "take the hill" or "move out", it was never for debate or conversation. Lives are at stake and you could place others in jeopardy because of the social relationship that existed prior to the command.

The reality is that sometimes God places people in your life to get on your last nerve!

In the corporate business environment the same is true; it may not be lives but it could result in loss of a client or an account. Employees and managers need to willingly embrace their position or status in order for harmony to occur. Unless those above you grant you permission to call them by their first name or certain liberties to do things, I recommend keeping things formal and professional. Realize of course, that once permission is granted toward the informal, it is difficult to go back to being formal.

As difficult as it may seem, each role, title or position must be willingly embraced. There may be times when you work with a peer that you don't get along with. It is vitally important that you embrace the fact that you two simply just don't get along. There is no need to force the issue, simply agree that you don't agree and move on! It takes a secure person to do this because it may be your nature to want everyone to get along with you because you are a wonderful person. The reality is that sometimes God places people in your life to get on your last nerve! They come to strengthen your patience and longsuffering.

I have come to the conclusion that I don't fit in with everyone, I wasn't designed that way and it's okay! I was always a little different that way. This is a way to overcome being offended. You will not always be included in their party or invited to sit at the "Cool kids table".

Overcoming Offenses

Luke 17:1 says,

"It is impossible but that offenses will come, but woe to them through whom they come! It were better for him that a millstone were hanged about his neck, and he cast into the sea than that he should offend one of these little ones. Take heed to yourselves: If thy brother trespass against thee, rebuke him; and if he repent, forgive him."

If the punishment fits the crime, I would say that offending someone is a pretty serious crime. One way that offense comes is through the unwillingness to embrace the relationships that surround you.

Mark 4:15 provides another aspect of the nature of offense that can help us lead a victorious life.

> *When the word came, immediately Satan came to take away the word that was sown...* (those that have no root) (Gk: *Rhiza* = root for depth and stability) *in them. When affliction* (Gk: *Thlipsis* = trouble or pressure) *or persecution arises for the Word's sake, immediately they are offended* (Gk: *Skandalizo* = to cause a person to begin to distrust and desert one whom he ought to trust and obey).

What this passage tells us is that when people receive the Word of God, the enemy sets out to snatch it away from them before it takes root. So when affliction or persecution comes to present itself, the very word that they received which was designed to sustain them, because it did not take root in them, leads to them being offended and they begin to desert and distrust the one whom they ought to obey and trust.

Let me give you an example of how this dynamic unfolds in everyday terms.

In the home, it is easy to offend a family member or relative because of a misspoken word, an un-called for remark or simply playing around beyond one's comfort level. If the family is not close knit, division is inevitable.

Isn't it true that the very ones you love the most can hurt you the deepest? Every successful marriage that I know of has gone through times of deep hurt or disappointment because of what one person said to the other. The secret to success here is that they never let the words override their true love for each other. The phrase, "Charge it to my head and not my heart", is applicable here because everyone makes emotional mistakes.

In the church, all a minister has to do is speak against sin, and offence will rise like yeast rolls. Where people think they are spiritually strong, the conviction to correct a behavior, attitude or lifestyle in line with the Holy Spirit and the Word of God, is too close to home, and instead of "*receiving with meekness the engrafted Word which is able to save your soul*" (James 1:21b), many choose to be defensive and become offended.

The work place seems to be the easiest place to be offended because the nature of the environment is not solely about establishing and maintaining relationships within the work group, it is focused on providing a service to a customer or getting a product developed, marketed and delivered. It is not the priority of many supervisors to ensure that you are happy and that you like them. If you were a customer, that would be a different matter, but because you work for and with them in the company, you must embrace the fact that you are there to do a job, not establish relationship.

However, I have seen where in doing your job professionally, you can establish a relationship dynamic where all the defenses are pulled down and the "real you" can come out without fear of being cut down or perceived as weak.

I remember conversations with my director and VP in closed door sessions that had nothing to do with profit margins and sales quotas. It was in moments like these where I was able to share my testimony and the Word of God with these important individuals. They were real people who had real issues and needed a real Word from someone who knew the real God. I remember thinking "This is what I was really sent to do in this company", this is what makes it "divine", because I believed that God inspired and orchestrated me to be in that place, at that particular time. I knew that if the performance or execution of my duties was sub-par, they would not respect me enough to ask my opinion about anything, let alone want to hear anything I had to say about how good my God really is, and how He is a forgiving God who understands and cares about them and their family.

I also remember working in an environment where I was the only practicing Christian. I would complain in my heart about the gossip, backbiting and derogatory jokes I was subject to hearing on a daily basis. I would pray that God would send other Christians to the work center because I was tired of being the only one upholding the standards of the Bible. I had no one to share the gospel with other than the "Uncircumcised Philistines" I worked with daily. How ironic is that, no one to witness to other than sinners?

Over the course of a year, God answered my prayers one by one those unbelievers were replaced with Christians. I rejoiced when I heard that church-goers were now in the work center; which meant we could now change the radio station to something more edifying, no more lewd comments, no more dirty jokes and no more gossip. Much to my surprise, the jokes increased, the radio station stayed where it was and the gossip went to new heights!

I prayed that God would remove them and bring more sinners. Later that year, I received a promotion and He removed me instead. The problem was that I did not embrace the divinity of Him setting me in that environment for His good. The Biblical pattern for this relationship dynamic can be found in the lives of Joseph and Daniel. In both situations, these men were divinely placed in an environment to declare the kingdom message to those who were unbelievers.

Did you know that Jesus did most of His ministry work in the marketplace and not in the church?

- At the <u>wedding</u> in Cana, Jesus turned water into wine (John 2:1-11)

- At the <u>well</u> in Samaria, Jesus gave a Word of knowledge and changed her life (John 4)
- At the <u>pool</u> of Bethesda, Jesus healed a man that had an infirmity for thirty-eight years (John 5)
- At the <u>Sea</u> of Galilee, Jesus fed five thousand people with two fish and five loaves of bread (John 6)

There are many other stories to validate my point, I simply want you to know that each of these people had a great opportunity to be offended, but each instead chose to embrace the divinity of the moment and the miraculous took place. One more example... In II Kings 5, the captain of the Syrian army (Naaman) was struck with leprosy. Because he was a man of great honor and felt he deserved the best treatment available, he prepared himself to pay roughly $80,000 in silver and gold. When he arrived at the home of Elisha the prophet, Elisha wouldn't even meet him at the door. Instead, he sent word through his servant saying,

> *"Go and wash in the Jordan seven times, and thy flesh shall come again to thee, and thou shall be clean. But Naaman was wroth and went away, and said, Behold, I thought, He would surely come out to me, and stand, and call on the name of the Lord his God, and strike his hand over the place, and recover the leper. Are not Abana and Pharpar, rivers of Damascus, better than all the waters of Israel? May I not*

> *wash in them, and be clean? So he turned and went away in a rage."*
>
> II Kings 5:9-12

This was a perfect opportunity for Naaman to be offended, primarily because things didn't go the way he planned. Just like many of us, when things don't the way we plan, or when people upset our plans, it is easy to be offended and miss the divine opportunity to be blessed. If Naaman walks away in anger, he would never have received his healing. Thank God he had men around him who understood the season and times of change for their captain. They said,

> (v13) *"Sir, if the prophet had told you to do some great thing, wouldn't you have done it? So you should certainly obey him when he says simply go and wash and be cured!"* (NLT)

How embarrassing this must have been for Naaman, who is now stuck at the intersection of pride and sickness. As many of you know, the Jordan was not the cleanest body of water in the region, much to the contrary; it was one of the worst.

I believe this dynamic happens regularly to people who have a situation and when a Word comes to them that they do not want to willingly embrace, they get mad and walk away. In the end, the servants convince Naaman to dip in the Jordan as the Man of God had instructed. Miraculously, his flesh became as healthy as a baby's skin. Notice Naaman's new confession of faith in verse 15,

> "*...now I know that [there is] no God in all the earth, but in Israel...*"

In other words, the very word that he esteemed to be offensive is the very word he is now making bold proclamations about.

How many times do I wish people could see things with the end in mind? There would not be nearly as many people offended in and outside the church. They would be more apt to willingly embrace truth when it comes.

Here is a Word I spoke in my church a few years ago regarding offenses...

"The enemy comes to attack you to destroy the anointing of God on your life. He knows that if he can keep you off balance through offences, you will not focus on God's will for your life. The church will default to just having church services but not really having any effect or impact in the city. God is a God of impact. He has called you to be a church that impacts its community.

"Yes, you may want to get back at those who have offended you, even though you tried to do something good for someone else, but it is to no avail, vengeance is mine, saith the Lord, I will repay".

You ask, "Why did this happen to me? The answer is simple... because of the Word of God that dwells inside of you. If the devil can constipate you through being offended, you will not be willingly to release the blessings you were blessed with to be a blessing to others". Therefore I say unto you, Be free to release and speak life to those around you, be free in the joy of the Lord, be free to love your enemies, bless them that curse you, do good to them that hate you, and pray for them which despitefully use you, that you may be the children of your Father which is in heaven"

PRINCIPLES TO LIVE BY

- The Father has designed our success and prosperity according to our ability to embrace His will. The more we embrace Him, trust Him and agree with Him, the more He proves Himself strong on our behalf.

- Some of us need to be convinced that God can use us even with our faults, flaws, insecurities and bad habits.

- Faith, at its essence, is based on the Principle of Agreeing with God on matters that you cannot see with the natural eye, but on what God has spoken. You cannot walk in faith without walking in agreement.

- One reason why Role Conflict occurs in the family is because wives and mothers are trying to do what the man or husband was designed to do.

- Employees and managers need to willingly embrace their position or status in order for harmony to occur.

- Isn't it true that the very ones you love the most can hurt you the deepest?

Section 3

Every Healthy Relationship Must Be...

Freely Invested In

John 3:16, 17

"For God so loved the world that He gave his only begotten Son, that whosoever believeth in him should not perish but have everlasting life. For God sent not his Son into the world to condemn the world; but that the world through him might be saved"

Any relationship left to itself will grow stale and dry, if it is not invested in. Like everything else that God has created that is alive, it exists on the **Principle of Respiration**. This principle states that everything that God has created and is alive, has to breathe. Humans breathe in oxygen and breathe out carbon dioxide, plants and trees breathe in carbon dioxide and breathe out oxygen; this exchange of breaths blesses the enrichment of life for both, we call this process photosynthesis.

Just as we cannot breathe in only, we cannot we always receive only.

Plants cannot give fruit or buds, unless they have received water and sunshine. Just as we cannot breathe in only, we cannot always receive only. We would hyperventilate or asphyxiate if we didn't breathe in and out properly. In the natural, earth itself gives as it receives what is sowed into it. Practically speaking, you cannot expect a harvest unless something has been planted.

This principle simply states that everything that is alive has to breathe (plants, animals, fish and mankind). The Greek word, *atallagma* means, that which is given in place of another by way of exchange. Breathing is a means by which we stay alive – this is God's design for sustaining life.

According to *Webster's Dictionary.com*, the word, *Respire* means to inhale and exhale air for the purpose of maintaining life. The important point here is that everything that He created and is alive, is automatically integrated in a process of interaction with others.

In Genesis 2:7 we find these words,

"And the LORD God formed a man's body from the dust of the ground and ***breathed into it the breath of life. And the man became a living person".*** (emphasis added)

Another example is found in Ezekiel 37:9, 10 (NLT)

"Then he said to me, "Speak to the winds and say: `This is what the Sovereign LORD says: Come, O breath, from the four winds! Breathe into these dead bodies so that they may live again.' " So I spoke as he commanded me, and the wind entered the bodies, and they began to breathe. They all came to life and stood up on their feet--a great army of them."

One more example regarding Jesus is found in John 20:22

"And when he had said this, ***he breathed on [them], and saith unto them, Receive ye the Holy Ghost..."*** (emphasis added)

In all three of these scriptures, we find a similar pattern - that when God wanted something to live or continue, He breathed into it the Breath of Life and it lived.

It is amazing to me that life is consistent with the ability to breathe in and breathe out. A patient can have low brain activity but as long as they are on life support or artificial respiration, they are still considered alive. Life is in the breathing.

The dynamic of exchange justifies that when God wanted to redeem mankind unto Himself, the price of sin had to be paid for through the blood of Jesus. The cost of human life was expensive and Jesus paid it off in full. I Corinthians 6:20 says,

> *"For ye are bought with a price; therefore glorify God in your body and in your spirit, which are God's."*

The Father so loved the world that He gave... not another angel, not another prophet, but His only begotten Son. He made an investment in us, while we were in a sinful or backslidden state, so that we might obtain salvation and eternal life. The question becomes, "What could we give in exchange for this great salvation?" The answer is two-fold, everything and nothing. This is why the nature of divine relationships is so perplexing. It will cost you everything, in that, salvation will require you giving your life (body, soul and spirit) to Him, and nothing, in that, there isn't any amount of money that could pay for His saving grace.

Making an investment is God's natural way of keeping the cycle of life flowing. Terms like sowing, speaking, giving, and pouring are used throughout the scriptures to reflect God's divine nature for our continued deliverance, healing, prosperity and it, like the other two dynamics (Clearly Defined and Willingly Embraced) affect the three major arenas of our lives: family, church and in the workplace. In this section, we will look closely at the divine relationship dynamic established by God from the concept of Freely Investing in the relationships that surround you.

God has determined that mankind is worth saving, so the first thing we need to do is to remove the churchy notion that we are not worthy of His grace and mercy. He knows exactly what He's doing by counting us worthy of so great a salvation. No one could force Him to make the decision to pay for our ransom; He did it out of pure love for us!

> *"When we were utterly helpless, Christ came at just the right time to die for us while we were still sinners... But God showed his great love for us by sending Christ to die for us while we were still sinners."*
>
> Romans 5:6-8 (NLT)

Since we were created in the likeness of His image (Gen 1:26), we too, are designed to give out of the motivation of pure love just like He does. To the degree we give (time, money, energy, words) is the degree to which the relationship will grow. God designed things this way on purpose because He knows that in order to a relationship to continue, there has to be an investment.

Paul writes in II Corinthians 8:9 concerning Jesus Christ, *"For ye know the grace of our Lord Jesus Christ, that, though he was rich, yet for your sakes he became poor, that ye through his poverty might become rich."*

This scripture speaks to an investment that seemingly doesn't make sense. He took on poverty, so that we could become rich. It was the only way we could embrace the spirit of wealth and prosperity.

There are several scriptures that illustrate God's investment in mankind even when it doesn't make sense, or when the person is seemingly not qualified for the blessings they have received. In Luke 15, we see the Parable of the Prodigal Son. Here, we find a young man who demanded his inheritance from his father and then foolishly wasted it in a far away country. When he finally realizes the destitution of his situation he makes the decision to return back home and repent for making such a mess of his life. But while he was a far distance away, the father ran to him, fell on his neck, kissed him and rejoiced and said,

> *"Bring forth the best robe and put it on him and put a ring on his hand and shoes on his feet, bring the fatted calf and let's celebrate, for this my son was dead, and is alive again; he was lost, and is found. And they began to be merry."*

Notice that the Father's heart was to take the initiative and make an investment that would lead to restoration with his son, even if it did not make sense to the elder brother. The first investment here is the kiss. This kiss, as inappropriate as it may be in the work place, is perfectly appropriate when a covenant relationship is established. In normal dating relationships, the kiss takes the relationship to its next level, even if it is a simple peck on the cheek. It is the gesture that says, "Its OK to get a little closer". This is why it is commonly debated as to whether you should kiss on the first date (more on that later).

I believe the Father has kissed each of us who have accepted Jesus Christ as Lord because it speaks of restoration and acceptance.

Each investment gesture made by the Father in this story is significant and deserves some elaboration. The robe signifies the investment of covering, the ring signifies authority, the <u>shoes</u> symbolize son ship, (for only slaves walked around barefooted), and the <u>fatted calf</u> signifies a ceremonial sacrifice. I want to emphasize that it is the heart of the Father to initiate the investment. He willingly invests in that which He has created for the purpose of extending the relationship.

If more fathers would kiss their sons, there would be less division in the family and acceptance and validation would help them lead a more balanced life.

When I see my covenant brothers or sons in the faith, a handshake or hug simply will not do. Most of the time when I greet my biological sons Aaron (27) and Moshe (23), in private or in public, it is with a kiss. Even if we're in public at the gym where we all play basketball; we could be dripping in sweat and it is a handshake, hugs then I kiss them. Their friends often look at us in wonder because they have rarely seen a father figure to kiss their sons, as symbol of acceptance. I am not ashamed to express this toward them because I believe it is healthy and appropriate. If more fathers would kiss their sons, there would be less division in the family and acceptance and validation would help them lead a more balanced life.

When I see my father in the faith, Bishop Holcomb, he blesses me with "the Holy Kiss"; it is a statement of affirmation that says, "This is one of my sons". In many countries around the world, there is nothing strange about seeing a grown man kiss his sons or brothers. Actually, when I surveyed several women in the church as to what they thought when they see a father kiss their sons in the faith, or covenant brothers, they said it was beautiful to see and made a strong statement of belongingness.

One rule that I teach concerning freely investing in someone is that, you **never make an investment that is beyond what has been clearly defined between the two parties**. If what you are sacrificing goes way beyond the understanding and dimensions of your relationship, you risk being misunderstood, rejected or can spark an illicit relationship that is not of God. For example, if I were to give a sister in our church a very expensive diamond ring, this type of gesture goes way beyond the understanding of the pastor – member relationship.

MY TESTIMONY

After my wife and I started dating and going to church, we began to express our feelings for each other more openly. I wanted our dating relationship to go to the courting phase; I knew that words would not be enough! I had to make an investment. Even though I did not have a lot of money then, I knew that unless an investment was made commensurate with my level of commitment,

I would miss out on this divine moment to be lifelong partners. I purchased a little speck of a diamond ring from the Base Exchange on Langley AFB, Virginia. It would be embarrassing to look at now, but back then, it meant everything. It made the statement that said, "I am making an investment to back up what I have been saying". Thankfully, she said, "Yes", to my proposal and I slipped it on her finger. Mother Garrett's words were prophetic because on December 6, 1980, almost six months to the day, we were married.

ADVICE TO SINGLES

I advise singles to draw to ministries that endorse handling the courtship in the proper way. One suggestion the world offers is that of sexual experiences. This too, is an investment because it involves giving oneself and receiving what the other is willing to give up. The danger here is "Why buy the cow, when the milk is free?" Sex before marriage is a huge investment to make before getting married. I believe if a man tells a woman that he loves her, there ought to be an investment that parallels his statement. Young ladies should not buy into the deception of giving up something as precious as their virtue to a person who has made a minimal investment through words. Remember, precious ones, you are bought with a price!

I also teach singles that kissing on the first date can lead to misunderstanding that could falsely define the relationship. Any respectable young man or woman should know the dangers of misleading someone down the wrong path by opening the door of intimacy too soon. Some would say, "It's just a kiss, what's the big deal?" I would respond by saying, clearly define the relationship and embrace whatever level of exchange is appropriate first, before any lips touch.

Another way the world teaches this is through gifts of "bling bling". You cannot buy your way into a divine relationship; it comes by way of sacrifice. Many young women that I asked during a recent *Singles Sensation Conference* we hosted shared that having a man with money is not the number one criteria for marriage. It came in a close second. Please know that most of the young ladies had jobs of their own and were making money on their own already. Having a good heart and willingness to support them was the number one qualifier; interestingly, good looks came in third place!

This spoke volumes to me because it is important for young ones to embrace the understanding that a bride is for a day, but a wife is for life. You can still treat her like a bride however, which makes her feeling special and appreciated. A sacrificial offering is always appropriate when you want a relationship to develop or be restored. You cheapen it when you withhold what you should invest. This is God's way of exchange. Consider what King David said, in regard to building an altar for the purposes of giving offerings to the Lord.

> *"Then the angel of the LORD told Gad to instruct David to go up and build an altar to the LORD on the threshing floor of Araunah the Jebusite. So David went up to do what the LORD had commanded him through Gad. Araunah, who was busy threshing wheat at the time, turned and saw the angel there. His four sons, who were with him, ran away and hid. When Araunah saw David approaching, he left his threshing floor and bowed before David with his face to the ground. David said to Araunah, "Let me buy this threshing floor from you at its full price. Then I will build an altar to the LORD there, so that he will stop the plague."*
>
> *"Take it, my lord the king, and use it as you wish," Araunah said to David. "I will give the oxen for the burnt offerings, and the threshing boards for wood to build a fire on the altar, and the wheat for the grain offering. I will give it all to you." But King David replied to Araunah, "No, I insist on buying it for the full price. I will not take what is yours and give it to the LORD.* ***I will not present burnt offerings that have cost me nothing!"*** *So David gave*

> *Araunah 600 pieces of gold[b] in payment for the threshing floor.*

I Chr 21:18-24 (NLT, emphasis added)

David understood that if you want to establish a place of worship, it should cost you something. If it is free, then its value is diminished. When you sow, give or pay full price for something precious (like the threshing floor), you place a higher value on it. Worship is costly, but it leads to an exchange that is life changing and liberating. Tithing is simply giving God what is already His. The question becomes, "Can He trust you to give Him a tithe (tenth) of what He has given you?" When you tithe, you give God the opportunity to bless you to an overflowing abundance. I have many stories to share regarding God's restoration of family finances because we were obedient to Him concerning the tithe.

II Corinthians 9:6 (NLV) says,

> "*Remember, the man who plants only a few seeds will not have much grain to gather. The man who plants many seeds will have much grain to gather. Each man should give as he has decided in his heart. He should not give, wishing he could keep it. Or he should not give if he feels he has to give. God loves a man who gives because he wants to give. God can give you all you need. He will give you more than enough. You will have everything you*

> *need for yourselves. And you will have enough left over to give when there is a need.* The Holy Writings say, "*He has given much to the poor. His acts of love last forever.*"

Psalm 112:9 says

> ***It is God Who gives seed to the man to plant.*** *He also gives the bread to eat. Then we know He will give you more seed to plant and make it grow so you will have more to give away. God will give you enough so you can always give to others.* (emphasis added)

Did you see who initiated the process? God Himself does, by giving seed to those who will sow. This is what makes it a divine principle, because it is initiated by Him and then He watches over His Word to perform it. Multiplication and abundance come to those who sow or invest in God's purposes. Some may sow money, words, gifts, expressions of love and time; either way, they have seen and testified of the blessed opportunities that have unfolded right before their eyes. The key to sowing is this – You must do something to activate the process. Miracles will take place when you do this.

In II Kings 4 (NLT), we find a widow who is caught in deep debt, her husband has passed away, she has two sons, no job, no income and the creditors have come to take away her two sons as payment for her debts. This sounds like something that could easily be a 21st century story, doesn't it? Her resources were dried up, so there was no way for her to keep the process of exchange alive and keep herself out of debt. Here's what the prophet Elisha said,

> "*Borrow as many empty jars as you can from your friends and neighbors. Then go into your house with your sons and shut the door behind you. Pour olive oil from your flask into the jars, setting each one aside when it is filled." So she did as she was told. Her sons kept bringing jars to her, and she filled one after another. Soon every container was full to the brim! "Bring me another jar," she said to one of her sons. "There aren't any more!" he told her. And then the olive oil stopped flowing. When she told the man of God what had happened, he said to her,* ***"Now sell the olive oil and pay your debts, and you and your sons can live on what is left over."*** (emphasis added)

Without an opportunity to generate seed to sow, her part of the exchange process was hindered resulting in her being in debt. Thankfully the prophet was available (just as many others are placed in our lives by God) to activate the process by giving her something to get started. Notice that the oil ceased when she ran out of vessels to fill. I believe if she would have gotten more vessels the oil would have continued.

Now she has enough to begin an exchange, sell the oil, pay her debt and live. Not having something to give or unwilling to give will hinder the furtherance of your prosperity. Secular investment counselors will tell you that you have to have money in order to make money. You have to start the process somewhere, because this is the way God designed life. In the investment world it's called, "Start up capital".

This exchange process is as simple as breathing. You can't just breathe in all the time; you have to breathe out also. Similarly, you can't be a taker all the time or a giver all the time, there has to be an exchange in order for life to continue. People who are "takers only" self-centered people who never get to experience the fullness of a relationship. Someone once said, "Love isn't love unless you give it away". Ironically, you can't keep giving without receiving. Pastors and church leaders often experience this particular dynamic of giving of themselves until there is nothing left to give. Church members need to know that because their pastor is only human, they have to allow room (space and time) for their pastor to be refreshed. This is why attending conferences and retreats or a sabbatical is so vitality important for clergy. Once pastors get away from everything and everyone, they can step back and refocus on the vision, see things from a different perspective and renew their strength. Usually when I return from a conference, I am fired up, and loaded with fresh new insights, revelations and truths to pass on to my members. Because I have freely received, I can freely give.

The Bible makes a statement about investing in Matthew 6:21, it says,

> *"For where your treasure is, there will your heart be also."*

What Jesus was saying is that you put your money (treasures) in the things you cherish the most. You will notice that where you spend most of your money clearly shows where your priorities are. If the relationships that surround you are a priority in your life, then it is time to make an investment. It is dangerous to wait for others to initiate an investment. If it is on your heart to do so, go ahead, take the step and make a gesture of love toward someone you know God has placed in your life. You will be surprised at what a random act of kindness or expression of love will do. Let's take a look at this dynamic within the three areas that affect most of us – the church, the home and the workplace.

IN THE CHURCH

Genesis 2:7 says,

> *"And the Lord God formed man (Adam) out of the dust of the ground, and*

breathed into his nostrils the breath of life; and man became a living soul".

John 20:22 says, *"And when he had said this, he (Jesus) breathed on them, and said unto them, Receive ye the Holy Ghost."*

These two scriptures make powerful statements about freely investing life into someone. Just as Adam couldn't move without the breath of life infused into him and the disciples could not move in power without the Holy Ghost, we cannot move toward a healthy relationship with the Lord or with one another without a fresh breath of His spirit.

When the Word of God is spoken, sang or prophesied, life is invested into God's people. When church leaders preach, teach, counsel or correct someone in love they are actually speaking life into you. To the degree that you receive those words, in the degree to which you will be restored and refreshed. Jesus said in John 6:63b, *"The words I speak unto you, they are spirit and they are life."* Indeed, when the Son of God speaks the Word of God, spirit and life are birthed.

On the contrary, when the Word is given, if a person does not embrace it, they hinder their development relationship with their church relationship and the result is oftentimes stagnation. Imagine a preacher speaking profound truths and the congregation sits idling in lethargy and indifference. Where there are no *Amen's*, no confirming witness, no hands raised, this is a sure sign that there is something is wrong in the relationship dynamic of that church. The preached Word is given to stir the hearts of the hearers.

Hebrews 4:12 says,

> *"The Word of God is quick (alive) and powerful and sharper than any two-edged sword, piercing even to the diving asunder of soul and spirit, and of the joints and marrow, and is a discerner of the thoughts and intents of the heart."*

This scripture indicates that the Word of God goes to the essence of our being: body, soul and spirit. It is directed at getting us to the place of investing and receiving freely. All these are God inspired ways to invest in our lives so that we may live a prosperous and peaceable life.

MY TESTIMONY

Oftentimes, I hear testimonies from Christians regarding how someone in the church has blessed them with something unexpected. These blessings keep the church alive and enjoyable! Once, our school, Gateway Christian Academy, received an unexpected visit from the city health inspector. He wrote us up for not having proper serving equipment and commercial grade items in accordance with city health guidelines. We didn't know we needed these items at that time because all we were doing was heating up the sack lunches that the students brought from home. He said he would give us a few weeks to either get the equipment items needed or he would have to shut down our hot lunch program. I met with our Board of Directors and we began to pray. I also called a special PTA meeting to inform the parents that they may have to supply lunches for their children temporarily if we could not come up with the kitchen equipment by the inspectors deadline.

After the meeting, a parent came to me with an amazing offer. He said, "Pastor, don't shut down the hot lunch program. This school has been a blessing to my little girl and you all have been so good to my family, I want to be a blessing to the school... if it's okay with you." He said, "I am in the commercial kitchen business and we just finished a project for the Dallas Independent School District and upgraded the equipment in five of their schools. The equipment is still in great condition and we have no place to put it. We have commercial grade ovens, refrigerators, deep freezers and serving lines that I would like to donate to the school". Anybody who knows the cost of commercial grade equipment knows that items like these could easily sell for thousands of dollars each. I began to praise God for His divine provisions. He said he would have his men, deliver, set up and charge the systems with

Freon so we could continue to serve hot lunches to the children. When the deadline came, the health inspector was prepared to bring our program to a close, when much to his surprise, all the new equipment was in place and in inspection order.

God blessed this parent to be a blessing to us! This is how freely investing works; it keeps the cycle of blessings flowing and keeps the relationship alive.

ON THE HOMEFRONT

I remember many years ago, my mother, along with several other mothers in our neighborhood protested in favor of busing us to better schools outside the ghettoized schools in our neighborhood. At the time, I didn't know what all the fuss was about, and I didn't know why I had to leave my friends in P.S. 284 in Brooklyn, N.Y.; a school that lacked adequate books, had broken windows and "creative" writings on the walls. What could possibly be wrong here? I thought. I knew everybody and everybody knew me; I was on safe and familiar grounds. But she was so adamant about us being bussed out because she wanted something better for us, even if it didn't make sense at that time. She made a sacrificial investment. She could have gotten arrested for my sake. Thankfully, it never turned violent; it was a peaceful protest that eventually led to us making new friends and experiencing new ideas in learning in a new school. I will always be thankful for her investment (among many, many others) into my life. Without her, I would not be what I am today. She always made sure that we had enough food and clothing while living in the projects. It wasn't until I was a little older that I understood that while we were in school, she would go to clean the homes and care for the children of more affluent people in New Jersey and still make it back home in time to make dinner and care for us. I will always love her for that!

When I look at my wife and how she relates to my sons, I am sometimes in awe of her unwavering support and encouragement towards them. Being a man, I could easily tell them the best way to deal with a tough situation is to "Be a man and deal with it", but she has a way of investing hope and inspiration to them that goes beyond my understanding. In her eyes, they may not be perfect, but they are mine! This is a mother's love that reflects the heart of God. It transcends logic, to make an investment where no profit is expected and loves without expecting anything in return.

As a father, I love to impart wisdom and soundness into my sons. This, to me, is more valuable than money. I know that if they continue to receive, these things will be with them for the rest of their lives, and one day, they will be able to teach their children God's Word. I agree with what Solomon said,

> *"My child, never forget the things I have taught you. Store my commands in your heart. If you do this, you will live many years, and your life will be satisfying. Never let loyalty and kindness leave you! Tie them around your neck as a reminder. Write them deep within your heart. Then you will find favor with both God and people, and you will earn a good reputation."*
>
> Proverbs 3:1-3 (NLT)

Fathers should never have to struggle with making an in their family. Whether it is an investment of time (going to see the kids play sports or having family fun time), or resources (there is nothing better than dad's BBQ cooking) or presence (simply being available when it counts). All of these are investment opportunities that will bring glory to God and manifest His plan for solid family relationships. When tough times arise, the love of God spreads through a close knit family like the anointing oil. It is easier to see how divine their love is when the members stand together, pray together, embrace one another, and keep the unity of faith, hope and love alive. There is no social structure stronger than family on the entire planet. I believe this is true because God inspired the relational dynamic of family.

Many may not believe that their siblings are another type and shadow of the divine relationship dynamic, but it's true! The investment of a loving, caring brother or sister is invaluable to the development of all of us. Despite the arguments and fights, I would get into trouble because I would not "squeal" on my sisters. If one got into trouble, we would cover for each other. While being interrogated by our parents, we didn't budge in admitting guilt or blame in front of them. We would settle matters later when we were alone. I dreaded those times because I was usually the culprit and my sister Jean would pinch or poke me, Elaine would look at me with her "stare of death", as she showed me her huge, tightly balled up fist and Rene would just flat out say, "I'm gonna jack you up later, you just wait". I laugh at the thoughts of those times now, but back then, it was no laughing matter! Oddly, I see God was working a divine work between my sisters and me all the long.

I've seen the same thing happen with my sons. They cover for each other in such a matter they exemplify the Father's behavior that says, "I'll cover your sins" and bury them in the Sea of Forgetfulness.

I pray that the readers of this book will look closely at their families. See God at work in bringing your family closer through the investments you make in each other.

IN THE WORKPLACE

Believe it or not, but the workplace can be a place where the manifestation of God's provision can clearly be seen. Looking in the Bible, we find examples of people earning a living through farming, trading, and making clothes, tools, oils and the like. It was an agrarian society back then that gave God opportunities to move in their lives just as we need Him to move today. In the corporate setting, God takes pleasure in blessing His people in board rooms and cubicles just as He would bless them in the Bible days with rain, sunshine and fertile ground.

God reveals to Abraham His plan to bless the people who are obedient to Him. God says through Abraham,

> *"The Lord shall open unto thee his good treasure, the <u>heaven to give the rain unto thy land in his season</u>, and to bless all the work of they hands: and thou shall lend to many and thou shall not borrow."*
>
> Deuteronomy 28:12

This scripture addresses a special agricultural blessing that transcends into the work environment.

Most supervisors and managers would agree that a faithful, productive employee is worth investing in. When I worked in corporate America, I invested in departments and employees that were producing. It was easy for me to provide incentives for those departments that consistently made their quota, provided accurate reporting and had exemplary attendance. Their behavior blessed me (because it made me look good before my Director) and in turn, I would bless them with appropriate incentives. This kept the cycles of sowing and reaping alive in the work place.

When you sow good efforts, you reap the benefits of a healthy work environment. No one wants to go to a job when there is no enthusiasm and where it seems as though management does not care about the employees. However, when those in leadership invest in good people, it affects the attitude and the performance of all the workers in the department. I remember noticing that the moral in one of my departments was slipping; you could feel it as soon as you walked in the room. I asked the supervisor what was going on. She replied, "The evening shift was feeling left out because so many things were happening in the day time and they were getting recognition while the night shift people were feeling neglected".

My solution was to make an investment. I asked the Director to take a moment and visit the evening team, we threw a mini-party, ordered pizzas and Coke for everybody and after apologizing for not being there for them, we made a verbal commitment to pay more attention to them. The results were incredible! Reporting increased, creative recognition programs for "evening crew people only", were birthed and moral increased. Had we let the environment remain as it was, the work environment would have been unwholesome. One small investment of presence, a gesture of commitment and a few pizzas, turned the whole department around for the betterment of everyone.

This dynamic goes both ways. An employee can make an investment in the supervisor as well to keep the "cycle of life" going. Sometimes employees have ideas that management may neglect because of busy schedules or is skeptical that the idea will work. Employees can submit their creative ideas, suggestions and proposals in a manner that will make the supervisors take notice. This kind of feedback is healthy because it lets management know of situations that exists that they may not be aware of. Fixing a situation can be as easy as making an investment of ideas and recommendations to enhance the work environment.

If the supervisor willingly ignores a suggestion or idea, because of fear of a paradigm shift or because they are close-minded, they stifle the employer-employee relation. A neglected issue doesn't just go away; it reproduces itself in other areas. The very familiar adage, "Necessity is the mother of all inventions", is true. People have become millionaires because of a suggestion of idea that met a need. I teach the leaders in my church that the people who make the most money are those who are solving the biggest problems.

SOMETIMES GOD DOESN'T MAKE SENSE

One of the most intriguing points about the nature of divine relationships is that sometimes God doesn't make sense. The quality of a relationship is defined by the investment made into it. What I did not understand for a long time is that the relationships in my life were inspired by God. Good ones, bad ones, some long term, some brief, some stressful, while others were a blessing. It wasn't until God gave me a revelation of what He was doing as far as relationships, that I truly understood why certain people were in my life and a particular time. This revelation changed everything.

> *"For my thoughts are not your thoughts, neither are your ways my ways saith the Lord, For as heavens are higher that the earth, so are my ways higher than your ways and my thoughts higher than your thoughts."*
>
> Isaiah 55:8

Here, the Lord gives us a simile of how His methods and reasons for surrounding us with people who try our patience beyond our comprehension. He places us in situations where we can only ask ourselves, "*How did I wind up in this situation?*" It doesn't make any sense on one hand and it makes perfect sense on the other. The scriptures are filled with stories that made no sense to me. Why would God make such an investment of protection, promises and provisions to a people who were reprehensible? If is it true that the quality of a relationship is defined by the investment made into it, He must really think highly of us to give us more chances than we deserve to get things right.

I believe God's revelation is man's invitation to get involved with what He is already involved in. He gives us a revelation of being the God of second and third chances so we can give others second and third chances to reconcile the broken relationships in our lives. In the same manner He forgave the children of Israel for their negative behavioral cycles, He will forgive us. Their cycle of belief and unbelief followed by belief again, was almost predictable. They would obey God, He would prosper them, they would become arrogant, and turn to other gods, calamity would come, wars would ensue, they would repent, cry out unto God, make appropriate sacrifices, and He in turn, would forgive them, protect them from their adversaries, heal their land and point them toward a prosperous life again, only for the cycle to repeat itself for centuries. It doesn't make sense does it?

Here's what He showed me regarding His people and taking the initiative toward right-standing with Him.

1. **His nature is to take the initiative**. Usually the person who wants the

relationship to work is the person who takes the first step toward a healthy relationship.

2. **The starting point for taking initiative is desire and passion**. Initiative is defined simply as, *the first move*, according to the Webster Illustrated Contemporary Dictionary. God has a desire and a passion for us to be reconciled to Him, even if it doesn't make sense to others. He will always take the first move toward us. His ultimate move was sending His only begotten Son, Jesus Christ.

3. Initiators are not afraid to take a risk for something they want. There is a cost for this action, but there is a greater cost for inaction. Proverbs 18:24 says,

> *"A man that has friends must first show himself friendly"*.

To summarize these points, I will say that God was true to His own nature by having a desire and passion toward us by sending Jesus Christ who would freely give His life as a ransom for many. (Mark 10:45) Since we were created in His image, it should be part of our nature to make the first move toward forgiveness to a person who is hurting, you will be surprised what a random act of kindness will do in the workplace as well as in the home or at church.

I pray that this book will cause you to look carefully at the people in your life and those that surround you. Go ahead, no one is looking. Ask yourself, "Why is this person in my life at this time – is it for a reason, a season or a lifetime?"

Ask yourself, "Is our relationship clearly defined? (friend or foe? blessing or test?)"

Is the relationship willingly embraced, in other words, are all parties concerned okay with the definition of the relationship? If not, somebody has to ask the difficult questions that will cause each to honestly look again at the dynamics of your relationship.

Ask yourself, "Who is making the investments in this relationship and is it commensurate with the previous two steps?" If there is no mutual investment made, someone should determine how healthy the relationship is, because as a living testimony, everyone involved must give and receive.

PRINCIPLES TO LIVE BY

- Making an investment is God's natural way of keeping relationships flowing.

- To the degree we give (time, money, energy, words) is the degree to which the relationship will grow. God designed things this way on purpose because He knows that in order for a relationship to continue, there has to be an investment.

- A sacrificial offering is always appropriate when you want a relationship to develop or be restored. You cheapen it when you withhold what you should invest

- A mother's love reflects the heart of God. It transcends logic, it makes an investment where no profit is expected and loves without expecting anything in return

- Your workplace can be a place where the manifestation of God's provision can clearly be seen

- When you sow good efforts, you reap the benefits of a healthy work environment. No one wants to go to a job when there is no enthusiasm and where it seems as though management does not care about their employees.

A PRAYER FOR THE RELATIONSHIPS THAT SURROUND YOU

Father, I come boldly before you in the name of Jesus Christ lifting up the people you have placed in my life. First of all, I lift you up and I praise your Holy Name and I declare that you are worthy of all the praise I can utter. I thank you for giving me people in my life to encourage me, teach me and bless me on one hand and then I thank you for those in my life who are there to stretch me, correct me and even those who challenge me.

I embrace the idea that this is all your doing and that you know exactly what I need by way of relationships to keep me humble an yet confident to walk in the things you have prepared for me from the foundation of the world.

Father, I thank you for the concept of family and so I speak blessings over the members of my family. I pray that you will heal every broken family relationship and restore healthy and lasting relationships among us, so that the next generation will be supportive and in right standing with you and with one another.

In your wisdom, you have placed me in a good church, under a good pastor and I am surrounded by people who love me and support me and my family. I thank you for the Word of God being spoken into me as daily bread that nourishes my soul and refreshes my spirit.

I thank you for the people I work with on a daily basis. I speak the Peace of God to be in the workplace and I come against all manner of seditions, gossip, slander, backbiting and any ungodly acts that could hinder the balance of healthy relationships between my co-workers and me, in the Name of Jesus

Lastly, I pray for those who have been hurt by abusive relationships or those who been neglected for too long. I pray that forgiveness, and trust be restored in their lives and that You, Father God, would place trustworthy people in their lives so they can enjoy the uniqueness of others and laugh again.

I pray these things in Jesus' name. Amen!

For more information about Pastor Ralph Dawkins
or Christian House of Prayer - San Angelo call:
(325) 653-0418
Or
Visit our website at: www.chopsa.org

More material available by Pastor Dawkins

Standards of Christ

The Making of a Kingdom-Minded Church

A Clean Heart and Pure Intentions

The Principle & Power of Agreement

God's Revelation, Man's Invitation

Miracles Don't Come Easy

Made in the USA
Columbia, SC
21 October 2024